Adoption Law for Adopters

in England and Wales

Mary Lane

Adoption UK

Adoption UK was founded in 1971 as a support and self-help network for adoptive families. Now, as a national charity, it provides information, advice, support and training to prospective adopters, adoptive parents, long-term foster carers and special guardians. Its services include: a telephone helpline, local support groups, contact networks, magazines and publications, training programmes and courses, and an Online Community. In addition, it works with national and local governments to promote the concerns of adoptive families.

Dedicated to the memory of Daphne who died in 2005 – an adopted person and adoption professional as well as a friend who is much missed.

First published in 2006
by Adoption UK
46 The Green, South Bar Street, Banbury, Oxfordshire
OX16 9AB, UK

www.adoptionuk.org

Copyright © Mary Lane 2006

Cover and main pages design by Carrie-Louise Webb

ISBN: 978-0-9515950-2-2
            0-9515950-2-4
Printed and Bound in Great Britain by Hobbs the Printers Limited, Totton, Hampshire

British Library Cataloguing in Publication Data.
A catalogue record for this book is available from the British Library.

Contents

Introduction

Foreword by His Honour Judge Donald Hamilton

Adoption is special.

Few court orders have so far-reaching an effect as an adoption order. Unlike any other order about a child, an adoption order continues throughout life: it cannot be varied or discharged even during childhood. It creates new families and, in doing so, it dismantles old families.

Social workers have long appreciated the special character of adoption and in recent years this has also received increasing recognition in the courts. In the county courts, in which most orders are made, adoption is reserved to courts designated as adoption centres, each with a dedicated adoption officer in the court office and judges selected for the work.

It is sometimes suggested that all that a child needs is love. That is a fallacy. All adopted children need a special parental love and children from the care system (who make up the majority of adopted children) can often present special challenges to their adoptive parents. These considerations explain the need for thorough preparation and rigorous assessment of prospective adopters, thoughtful selection and (according to age) preparation of children who are to be adopted, careful matching of adopters with children and readily available post-adoption support. These requirements lie at the heart of good adoption practice.

This book provides a clear and succinct account of this and of the law of adoption generally. It reflects Mary Lane's rare combination of experience as a social worker, a lawyer and a trainer. She has written primarily for adopters but her work will also be of value to social workers and others. It has certainly enhanced my own understanding.

Above all, I hope that this book will help adopters to understand that they too are special.

Donald Hamilton
Adoption Judge, Birmingham County Court

Introduction

Adoption in the UK has altered dramatically over the past 60 years. Originally, adoption was almost exclusively concerned with the babies of unmarried mothers who, under societal pressures, gave up their children to be adopted by married couples. Now, there are very few relinquished babies, and the vast majority of adoptions are of children from the social services care system. Nearly 61,000 children were in the UK care system at any one time in 2005. Many of these children will be looked after by foster carers and most will go home to their parents. However, a significant number will not return to their birth families because of their inability to care for them. These children are likely to be either adopted or placed in long-term foster care or special guardianship. In 2005, approximately 3,800 children were adopted from the UK care system.

All adopted children suffer some form of trauma through being separated from their birth families, and the majority of those children will have been by abused or neglected before entering the care system. Because of this, many adopted children need help with their physical, emotional, and behavioural development, and present a unique set of challenges to their adoptive parents, who deserve and are entitled to support.

Due to these immense changes in adoption practice, adoption law has been modernised by replacing the Adoption Act 1976 with the Adoption and Children Act 2002. This Act was fully implemented on 30 December 2005. It makes the welfare of the child paramount in considering and making decisions about a child's adoption. The Act's intention is also to improve the performance of adoption agencies, and promote greater use of adoption for looked after children.

This book is a guide to adoption law in England and Wales following the Act's full implementation. There are some differences between English and Welsh law. The law described in this book is English law, with the most significant differences in Welsh law identified in the text.

Possible advantages for adoptive families

The Adoption and Children Act 2002 brings huge changes in both adoption law and practice which should, if applied correctly, provide many advantages for adopters and their children.

Support
Local authorities have a legal duty to assess and plan the support needs of children and adoptive families before matching and placement. These

are both financial and other needs, such as counselling and training. Local authorities also have a legal duty, on request by the adoptive family, to assess support needs at any time during the adopted child's childhood. (Chapters 4 and 9)

Reviews
Reviews of children in adoptive placement must be chaired independently of the social services or adoption agency team. The Independent Reviewing Officer (IRO) has a duty to 'progress chase' children's care plans and resolve problems. They could also help prospective adopters progress concerns about a local authority's lack of action or support etc. (Chapters 7 and 9)

The IRM
Potential adopters whom adoption agencies propose to turn down for approval or to terminate their approval can ask for the Independent Review Mechanism (IRM) panel to examine the agency's proposal. (Chapters 2 and 9)

Information about the child given to adopters
Earlier and more comprehensive information will be given to adopters about children before placement, in the Child's Permanence Report, as well as the opportunity to be consulted about support plans through providing prospective adopters with the Adoption Placement Report and the Adoption Placement Plan. (Chapters 3 and 4)

Contact
Prospective adopters must be consulted about contact arrangements for the child before placement, and these can be changed if necessary, including by adopters, during placement. (Chapters 3 and 6)

Decision making before adoption
Prospective adopters will have parental responsibility and so be legally entitled to make decisions about the child from placement (shared with the local authority and birth parents) until the adoption order is granted. (Chapter 7)

The adoption
Most adoption order applications will not be opposed by birth parents. (Chapters 3 and 8)

This book is intended as a source of information about adoption law principally for people adopting in England and Wales, at all stages in the process of building their family by adoption, including assessment and approval, during adoptive placements, and after adoption orders are granted. The focus is adoptions arranged through agencies - local authorities and registered adoption societies (also known as voluntary adoption agencies).

There are brief references to the law on stepparent, intercountry adoption and other non-agency adoptions, such as those by relatives.

Each chapter includes sections drawing out the implications of the law for agency adopters, and suggests avenues that adoptive families can take to ensure that agencies meet their legal obligations.

This book will also aid social workers, IROs, adoption panel members, health workers and other professionals, in understanding the new adoption law, particularly from the perspective of adoptive families, as well as children involved in adoption and their advisers and advocates.

A list of the most important legislation – Acts, Regulations and Statutory Guidance, is in Appendix 1. It is outside of the scope of this book to describe other aspects of adoption, such as the social work processes in assessment, matching, introductions, placement and so on. Suitable resources on these topics are contained in the reading list.

This book should not be regarded as legal advice, which will depend largely upon the particular circumstances of the families involved, and may require consultation with a lawyer competent in adoption law.

The author's suggestions on possible implications arising from the new law are based upon her experience as a legal consultant to Adoption UK, to local authorities and registered adoption societies, and a long previous career in adoption social work and as a children's guardian and reporting officer.

Explanation of terms used

Adoption law, like all legislation, has its own set of legal terms and language. The main legal terms are set out below. In addition to these, in this book, references to 'prospective adopters' includes single adopters. Similarly, references to 'the child' includes children in sibling groups who are placed together in adoptive families.

Parental Responsibility
This is defined by the Children Act 1989 as "all the rights, duties, powers and responsibilities which by law a parent has in relation to a child and their property." In other words, the legal entitlement to make decisions about a child – names, education, medical treatment etc. For birth parents and guardians only, parental responsibility is the legal entitlement to give or withdraw consent to a child's placement for adoption, and to making adoption orders.

Mothers acquire parental responsibility for their children immediately on their birth. A father acquires parental responsibility by being married to the birth mother before or after the birth or, from 1 December 2003, by being jointly registered with the mother on their child's birth certificate. Unmarried fathers can also acquire parental responsibility by formal agreement with the mother, by a parental responsibility order or, very rarely, by an adoption order.

Agency adopters acquire parental responsibility (shared with the local authority and with the child's birth parents) when a child over six weeks of age is placed with them for adoption by an agency. Adopters acquire sole parental responsibility when an adoption order is granted by the courts.

Parents and Guardians

In adoption law, 'parent' means each birth parent with parental responsibility and includes adopters after an adoption order is granted. 'Guardian' means a legal guardian appointed after a parent's death, or a special guardian.

Fathers without parental responsibility

A birth father without parental responsibility is not automatically a party to court proceedings for placement and adoption orders, and is not entitled to give, withhold or withdraw his consent to his child being placed for adoption, or to seek the court's leave to oppose the making of an adoption order. However, under Articles 6 and 8 of the European Convention of Human Rights, courts are likely to be sympathetic to an application by a birth father without parental responsibility to be made a party to court proceedings about his child.

Where a father does not have parental responsibility, but his identity is known to the adoption agency, and the agency is satisfied that it is appropriate to do so, it must consult and advise him about his child being placed for adoption, and find out if he is intending to acquire parental responsibility, or apply for a residence or contact order.

Relatives

In the ACA 2002, a 'relative' means grandparent, brother, sister, uncle or aunt (by full or half blood), or by marriage or civil registration. This definition does not include great aunts or uncles or great grandparents.

Residence orders - Section 8 Children Act 1989

A residence order determines with whom a child lives. The holder of a residence order is given parental responsibility for the child, shared with the birth parents. Apart from the issue of residence, entitlement to make decisions is shared equally with the parents with parental responsibility. A residence order discharges a care order, so the child will no longer be in local authority care. The legal identity of the child does not change – they remain legally the child of their birth parents. Their nationality or immigration status also does not change.

Under previous law, unmarried couples could not adopt jointly – only one of the couple could be granted an adoption order. The partner of the adoptive parent was granted a residence order, so that they would have some parental responsibility. From 30 December 2005, unmarried or non-civil registered couples can adopt jointly – a residence order is now no longer needed.

Special Guardianship orders - Section 14 Children Act 1989
This is a 'halfway house' between a residence order and an adoption order. It gives parental responsibility to the special guardians, shared with the birth parents, but allows the special guardians to exercise parental responsibility to the exclusion of birth parents on most issues. However, the special guardians cannot cause the child to be known by a new surname or removed from the UK for more than three months without the leave of the court, or the written permission of each parent with parental responsibility. As with residence orders, the legal identity of the child does not change, they remain the child of their birth parents, and their nationality and immigration status does not change.

A special guardianship order is more permanent and secure than a residence order. Birth parents need to have the court's permission to apply to discharge a special guardianship order, and will only get this if there has been a significant change in circumstances since the order was made, and the court considers that the welfare of the child requires permission to be given. A special guardianship order discharges a care order – so the child will no longer be in local authority care, but it is not discharged by the granting of a care order.

Looked after children
Children are 'looked after' if a local authority is providing them with care and accommodation. Looked after children include those 'accommodated' under section 20 of the Children Act 1989. 'Accommodation' is a voluntary arrangement between local authorities and parents. Children subject to care orders, interim care orders or emergency protection orders are 'in care' and 'looked after'.Children offered to adopters by local authorities are looked after children who have been authorised to be placed for adoption (chapter 3).

Non-agency adoptions
These are adoptions of children by their stepparents or relatives which have not been arranged by agencies. It is illegal in the UK for a parent to place a child directly for adoption with anyone except a close relative.

Non-agency adoptions can include private foster carers (unrelated to the children) who apply to adopt them with or without the consent of their parents or guardians, and local authority approved foster carers who apply to adopt without the support of the local authority looking after the children. The ACA 2002 provides legal alternatives to stepparent adoption, and places some legal limitations to unrelated foster carers and relatives adopting (chapter 8).

Agency adoptions

There are two kinds of agency adoptions:

Children relinquished for adoption

Along with a handful of registered adoption societies, local authority adoption agencies are the providers of services for birth parents wishing to relinquish their child for adoption. Usually these children are babies and cared for in foster homes until adoptive placements are found, although some are placed with adopters within a few days or weeks of birth (chapter 3).

There are very few babies relinquished for adoption, and there is usually a long waiting list of prospective adopters. However, sometimes babies are relinquished for adoption because they have significant physical or learning disabilities, and registered adoption societies may be asked by local authorities to find adoptive families for these babies.

Children in local authority care authorised to be placed for adoption

These are usually older children, and have been removed from their birth families because of abuse and neglect, or the risk of it, and being returned to their families is not considered to be in their best interests. In rare cases, they are children who have been abandoned or orphaned. The legal circumstances of children available for adoption are set out in chapter 3.

CAFCASS (Children and Family Court Advisory and Support Service)

This is a national public body for England that provides children's guardians and family court reporters who safeguard and promote the welfare of children involved in family court proceedings. CAFCASS is accountable to the Department for Education and Skills. CAFCASS is independent of the courts, social services, education and health authorities. In Wales this service, on similar terms to CAFCASS, is governed by the National Assembly – with Welsh Family Proceedings Officers.

Abbreviations

Where legislation is referred to a number of times in the book, the following abbreviations are used:

AAR 2005 – Adoption Agencies Regulations 2005
ACA 2002 – Adoption and Children Act 2002
ASSR 2005 – Adoption Support Services Regulations 2005
CA 1989 – Children Act 1989
SAR 2005 – Suitability of Adopters Regulations 2005

Adoption services

Adoption services in England and Wales are provided by local authorities and registered adoption agencies. Any unregistered organisations or private individuals providing adoption services are acting illegally. All adoption agencies must comply with regulations and statutory guidance that cover in detail how these services must be provided.

Local authority adoption services

Local authorities in England and Wales have a legal duty to provide a comprehensive adoption service to people living in their area. The service must be designed to meet the needs, in relation to adoption, of the following groups: children, their parents and guardians, persons wishing to adopt a child, and adopted persons, their parents, birth parents and former guardians (ACA 2002, Section 3).

The adoption service provided by local authorities must include arrangements for the adoption of children, assessment and approval of adopters and the provision of adoption support services to adoptive families. Each local authority must prepare a plan for the provision of their adoption service, and this plan must be publicly available and kept under review.

A local authority may arrange for some of their adoption services to be provided by registered adoption and adoption support agencies, such as Adoption UK.

A local authority adoption service must be provided in conjunction with their other social services and with registered adoption agencies in their area, so that services are planned and delivered in a coordinated manner without duplication, omission or avoidable delay.

Adoption services provided by registered adoption societies (also known as voluntary adoption agencies or VAAs)

Registered adoption societies provide services which aim to complement local authority services by offering a specialist service recruiting, assessing, approving and supporting adopters for children who are looked after by local authorities and for whom local authorities have difficulty in finding suitable families.

Charging for adoption services

Most adoption services provided by local authorities and registered adoption agencies are free.

However they are entitled to charge for the assessment and approval of people wishing to adopt from abroad, and for providing pre and post-adoption reports to the child's country of origin.

Adoption panels

Adoption panels are part of the 'quality control' of the work of adoption agencies. Panel members, at least four of whom (including the chair) are independent of the agency, scrutinise the work of the agency and use their professional expertise or personal experience of adoption, to bring objectivity and provide advice to the agency decision maker about the approval of prospective adopters, whether children should be placed for adoption, and matches between children and prospective adopters. Adoption panels are also a 'sounding board' for agency social workers when tricky issues arise.

Each adoption agency must have at least one adoption panel. Large local authorities and registered adoption societies can have more than one panel and two or more small agencies can have joint panels.

Panel members

There must be no more than 10 panel members (11 in a joint panel), including :

a) A chair of panel (independent of the agency and with the necessary skills and experience).

b) Two social workers each with at least three years relevant post-qualifying experience (who may or may not be employees of the agency).

c) A director or other manager of a registered adoption society, or one (elected) member of a local authority adoption agency.

d) The medical adviser to the adoption agency, who must be a registered medical practitioner.

e) At least three independent persons including, where reasonably practicable, at least two persons with personal experience of adoption.

In a registered adoption society a person may not be an independent panel member if they are, or have been within the last year, a trustee or employee, or are related to an employee of the agency.

In a local authority adoption agency a person cannot be an independent panel member if they are, or have been within the last year, employed by that authority in their children and family social services department, are related to an employee, or is or has been within the last year a member of that authority. ('Related' here means a member of the same household, as well as related by blood, marriage or civil registration.)

A person cannot be an independent panel member if they are the adoptive parent of a child who was placed for adoption by that agency, unless the adoption order was made a year or longer ago.

A vice chair must be appointed by the agency from the members of panel to act if the chair of the panel is absent or the office is vacant. The vice chair need not be independent of the agency, although it is considered good practice that they should be.

The legal adviser to an adoption agency can be a panel member but this is not required by regulations.

Tenure of office of panel members

Members of adoption panels hold office for a term not longer than three years, and cannot hold office for the same adoption panel in the same agency for more than three terms – a maximum of nine years. A member of an adoption panel may resign at any time by giving one month's notice in writing to the agency. The medical adviser member of the adoption panel holds office for so long as they are the medical adviser.

If an adoption agency considers that any member of the adoption panel is unsuitable or unable to remain in office, it may terminate their office at any time by giving notice in writing with reasons.

Panel quorum

An adoption panel needs at least five of its members, including the chair or the vice chair, and at least one of the social workers and one of the independent members, to be able to meet as the panel. (For joint panels the quorum is six, including the same essential members)

Panel minutes

An adoption panel must make a written record of its proceedings, its recommendations and the reasons for its recommendations.

Panel advisers

The adoption agency must appoint a senior member of staff to help with the appointment, termination and review of appointing panel members. They are also responsible for the induction and training of panel members, for liaison between the agency and the adoption panel, and for monitoring the performance of panel members and the administration of the adoption panel. They also give advice to the adoption panel when requested, either generally or in relation to a specific case.

The agency adviser must be a registered social worker and have at least five years relevant post-qualifying experience and, in the opinion of the adoption agency, relevant management experience.

The statutory duties and functions of adoption agencies and adoption panels

The functions of adoption panels and the statutory duties of adoption agencies towards children, prospective adopters, matches between adopters and children, supervision and reviews of adoptive placements and adoption support are set out in the relevant chapters.

Ensuring standards in adoption agency work

National Minimum Standards for Voluntary Adoption Agencies in England and Wales and Local Authority Adoption Services in England

There are standards and regulations for the management, conduct and staffing of voluntary adoption agencies in England and Wales and for local authority adoption services published by the Department for Education and Skills. They form the basis of the framework under the Care Standards Act 2000 for the registration and inspection of adoption agencies in England and Wales, by the Commission for Social Care Inspection (CSCI) in England and by the National Assembly in Wales.

For example, each adoption agency must have a statement of purpose that sets out the aims and objectives of the service and a children's guide, and services must be carried on in a manner that is consistent with this statement. There are provisions governing the qualifications and suitability of the managers of the services, the way services are conducted, arrangements for the protection of children, staffing and suitability of workers, the keeping of the records, and complaints procedures.

Inspection reports by the CSCI of adoption agencies are available from their website (www.csci.gov.uk)

Adoption panels also provide scrutiny of the work of adoption agency social workers in individual cases.

The Independent Review Mechanism

This was established by the DfES in 2004 to provide independent reviews for prospective adopters whose agencies propose not to approve them or propose to terminate their approval, and enables those proposals to be reviewed by an independent panel (See chapter 3).

The quality of adoption social workers

The Restriction on the Preparation of Adoption Reports Regulations 2005 limit the persons who may prepare adoption reports in four main areas; about the suitability of a person to adopt a child, on whether a child should be placed for adoption, about matching a child with adopters, or about the making of an adoption order for a child.

These persons must be registered social workers employed by a local authority or registered adoption society, or acting on behalf of that local authority or a registered adoption society, and have at least three years post-qualifying experience in child care social work, including direct experience of adoption work, or supervised by a social worker with such experience.

A student social worker on an accredited training course, supervised by a suitably qualified and experienced social worker, may also prepare these reports. These regulations apply to reports prepared both in domestic and intercountry adoption.

Perhaps surprisingly, officers of CAFCASS or the Welsh Assembly who prepare court reports in adoption and placement court proceedings are not required to have direct adoption experience.

It is illegal for independent social workers (even registered and suitably qualified and experienced), to prepare adoption reports under the Adoption Agencies Regulations, unless they are acting for registered adoption agencies and supervised by them.

1

Becoming adopters – Eligibility, assessment and approval

Eligibility

The 'entry point' for becoming an adopter is meeting the legal eligibility criteria for being granted an adoption order. Clearly, if a person is not eligible, there is no point in pursuing the plan to adopt. Fortunately, eligibility is not difficult to achieve for most potential adopters. The ACA 2002 has amended the eligibility criteria to make them inclusive of more potential adopters. Specifically, couples can now adopt jointly, whether they are of the same or different genders, and whether or not they are married or civil registered.

The eligibility criteria

These criteria apply to all potential adopters, regardless of whether they are agency and non-agency prospective adopters.

Age

Prospective adopters must be at least 21 years old to be granted an adoption order, except that a birth parent adopting their own birth child may be 18 or over (likely to be very rare under the new law). There is no legal upper age limit.

Adoption by a couple

Couples, whether of the same or different genders, and whether or not married, or civil registered, may adopt jointly.

Adoption by one person

A single person may adopt, but a married or civil registered person cannot adopt without their married or civil partner unless there are special circumstances.

Adoption by a stepparent

The partner of a birth parent, whether or not they are married to or civil registered with the birth parent, can adopt their partner's child. The adoption order to the stepparent will give them the same parental responsibility as their birth parent partner, which they will then share equally; but the adoption order will terminate the parental responsibility held by the other birth parent.

Legal alternatives to stepparent adoption

The ACA 2002 provides alternatives to stepparent adoption which allow a stepparent who is married or civil registered with a birth parent, to acquire and share parental responsibility for the child by agreement with the other parents with parental responsibility (this is a written agreement which must formally made, witnessed by a court officer, and registered in court).

If that agreement cannot be reached, the married or civil registered stepparent can acquire responsibility by a court granting a parental responsibility order under Section 4A, Children Act 1989. Before applying for a stepparent adoption, married or civil registered couples might consider if an agreement to share parental responsibility would be better for the child than adoption – so that the child's legal relationship with one of their birth parents does not end. The court considering the application for a stepparent adoption and the assessing social worker will consider these alternatives with the welfare of the child, throughout their life, their paramount concern.

Domicile or Habitual Residence

A single person (or one of a couple) must be domiciled in the UK, Channel Islands or Isle of Man, or each applicant must have been habitually resident in any part of the British Islands for at least one year preceding the making of an adoption order.

Domicile

A person is domiciled in the country in which they either have or is deemed to have their permanent home. A person can only have one domicile at any time. A person acquires a domicile of origin at birth which remains their domicile, wherever they go, unless a new domicile is acquired (a domicile of choice). A person may acquire a domicile of choice by residing in a country other than that of their domicile of origin with the intention of residing there indefinitely.

2

Habitual Residence

This depends on the quality of residence, not just duration, and requires an element of intention. Residence must continue for some time, but there is no requisite period of residence that establishes it as habitual. Factors such as owning property, type of employment contract, financial arrangements, location of bank accounts, and local connections may be relevant in deciding if someone has habitual residence. Someone who leaves the UK to take up employment elsewhere may acquire habitual residence in another country, but they may also retain habitual residence in the British Islands because of the links they have maintained (those listed above). It is possible to be habitually resident in two countries at the same time.

Eligibility to adopt from overseas

Eligibility to obtain an adoption order in England or Wales for a child from another country also requires that the adopters comply with the law and eligibility criteria that operate in that country. For example, some countries do not accept single or gay adopters.

Suitability to adopt

Suitability of non-agency adopters

Stepparent, relative or private foster carer adopters, intercountry adopters and local authority foster carers applying to adopt without the support of the local authority, must be eligible to be granted an adoption order according to the criteria above. Apart from intercountry adopters, they will usually have been carers for a child before the issue of adoption arises, and the assessment of their suitability to adopt begins when they notify their local authority of their intention to apply for an adoption order, at least three months before they apply. Apart again from intercountry adopters, there is no legal requirement that non-agency adopters be approved by an adoption agency.

The assessment of their suitability to adopt that particular child is undertaken by a suitably qualified social worker from the local authority. This social worker advises the court in the report they prepare about whether the assessment is positive. However, the court can decide that an adoption order should be made even if the social worker does not recommend it. The court's decision will depend on what is in the best interests of the child, based on all the circumstances.

Criminal Records checks for non-agency adopters

The local authority is required to obtain a CRB (Criminal Records Bureau) check to see if the non-agency applicant, or any adult members of the household, has any criminal convictions or cautions for offences which might throw doubt upon their suitability to adopt a child. However, having convictions or cautions for such offences does not automatically prohibit a non-agency adopter from being granted an adoption order. The court, taking into account the local authority's report, will decide whether or not the adoption order, in all the circumstances, is in the best interests of the particular child.

Suitability of agency adopters

Whether or not a person is suitable to adopt a child is largely a matter for assessment and judgement by the panel and the agency, prior to any child being placed, of their personality, reaction to life experiences, attitudes, parenting abilities, domestic circumstances, health etc. The focus is on whether they can meet the emotional and physical needs of a child, and give them safe care. Adoption agencies must offer people interested in adoption information, counselling and preparation in accordance with the regulations and guidance set out below. If the agency decides to progress the application, it must then undertake a detailed assessment of their suitability.

Adoption Guidance – agency adopters

Recruitment

Adoption agencies must develop a plan for recruiting and preparing prospective adopters who can meet the needs of children waiting for adoption. When developing this plan, agencies should take into account past trends, anticipated needs, local consortia plans and information from research and the National Adoption Register. This Register collects information about children needing adoption in England and Wales, and approved prospective adopters.

The plan should help agencies focus recruitment on groups of prospective adopters and prioritise applications according to the needs of children waiting for adoption. Applicants should be told how agencies prioritise applications.

Where there is a delay to timescales required in statutory guidance (below) or there are additional timescales set by agencies, the reasons for these should be explained to the applicants. They should also be kept informed of progress in relation to their case.

Informing and counselling prospective adopters

Adoption guidance (statutory) requires that when a couple or an individual contacts an agency and indicates an interest in adopting, the agency should respond impartially and promptly (AAR 2005, 21). Agencies should provide them with general written information about adoption, children who need adoptive families, the agency's expectations of adopters, and where to obtain further information from them or other agencies.

Local authorities have a duty under the ACA 2002 to provide, or arrange to provide, domestic and intercountry adoption services. If a local authority is not able to provide a service to potential intercountry adopters it must direct the applicants to an agency who can. Local authorities and registered adoption societies can charge for an assessment of potential intercountry adopters (known as a 'home study') and pre and post-adoption reports to the child's country of origin, where they are required.

If a VAA is not registered to provide an intercountry adoption service, it should offer general information about adoption and provide details of agencies which can provide an intercountry adoption service. If the agency has specific selection criteria for domestic adopters based on particular religious beliefs, applicants should be informed and, if necessary, be referred to another agency.

Applicants for approval as adopters must not be automatically excluded on the grounds of age, health or other factors, except in the case of certain criminal convictions or cautions (see below), or if they are not eligible to apply for an adoption order (see above). However, adoption agencies are not obliged to accept an assessment application from every prospective adopter who has received information and preparation. For example an application may be declined from those who are only interested in adopting a child the agency is not able to place with them or where their preparation reveals unrealistic or inappropriate expectations about adoption, or they would be unlikely to be safe carers.

Foster carers who express an interest in adopting children in their care should be given advice about the procedures that will apply in their case. (See adoption by foster carers in chapter 8).

Timescales for enquiries, applications and assessment

Agencies must adhere to these timescales set out in statutory guidance unless there are exceptional reasons. After a prospective adopter makes a first enquiry, written information about the adoption process should be sent to them by the agency within five working days. Within two months of their first enquiry, prospective adopters should be invited to an adoption information meeting or otherwise given information.

Agencies are required to prepare prospective adopters for the task of adoption and to offer them confidential counselling with experienced social workers. Agencies aim to ensure that prospective adopters receive as much information, preparation and counselling as is necessary for them to understand what adoption is likely to mean for them – the lows as well as the highs – and have a realistic understanding of the kind of children who need adoptive families. This is so that the prospective adopters can decide if adoption is really what they want, as well as whether they are likely to be suitable, before the formal assessment begins.

Agencies will ask prospective adopters to state if they have any significant health problems, or any criminal convictions and to consent to medical, Criminal Records Bureau and other checks required by law (see below). Many agencies will not offer their application form until the result of these checks are known.

The adoption panel's recommendation about the suitability of prospective adopters should be made within eight months of the receipt of their formal application for assessment. This eight month period begins when the completed application is returned to the agency, and entitles the prospective adopters to be assessed and considered by the adoption panel, unless they withdraw their application or an application is terminated because a specified offence is revealed (see below).

Implications for prospective adopters

Adoption agencies want to ensure during these initial stages of information giving, preparation and counselling, before the formal application for assessment is made, that their resources are used to assess prospective adopters who are most likely to be suitable. Agencies are not obliged to accept an application from every potential applicant for assessment.

For example, an application form will not be provided if the agency considers that the potential applicants are unlikely to be able to parent the kind of children for whom they are recruiting families, where their preparation and counselling reveals unrealistic or inappropriate expectations about adoption, or the checks reveal that they are not likely to be safe carers.

Entitlement to a review of an agency's suitability decision

Once the assessment has started, and unless the prospective adopters withdraw, or an application is terminated because a specified offence is revealed, their assessment must be presented to the agency's adoption panel. If after a panel recommendation the agency proposes not to approve applicants, prospective adopters are entitled to request an IRM review (see below). The agency's proposal as to whether the prospective adopter should be approved as suitable to adopt should be taken within seven working days of the adoption panel's recommendation. The prospective adopter should be informed orally of the agency's proposal within two working days and written confirmation should be sent within five working days.

Specified criminal offences prohibiting agency approval

Adoption agencies are required to obtain an enhanced criminal record certificate from the Criminal Records Bureau (CRB) for each applicant and adult members of their household (AAR 2005, 23). Applicants will be asked to consent to this at an early stage. Guidance suggests that ideally these checks should be completed before the agency starts the assessment of the prospective adopters. In practice this may not be possible due to delays in completing the checks, and so for some applicants the agency may decide that assessment proceeds in parallel with them.

However, the assessment should not be concluded and presented to the adoption panel until the CRB checks have been completed, as an adoption agency may not consider a person suitable to adopt a child, if they or any member of their household aged 18 or over:

(a) has been convicted of a specified offence committed at the age of 18 or over; or

(b) has been cautioned in respect of any such offence which, at the time the caution was given, they admitted.

Members of the household include lodgers, unless they live in accommodation within the building that is permanently separated by a locked door from the main household.

Specified offences include nearly all crimes against children and some sexual offences against adults. These are set out in the AAR 2005. The offence of 'common assault' on a child (a minor assault not involving bodily injury) is not a specified offence, and neither are offences committed before the applicant or household member was 18 years old, or non-sexual offences of violence against adults. The latter however may well affect judgements about suitability to adopt.

Where an adoption agency becomes aware that a prospective adopter or a member of their household has been convicted or cautioned for a specified offence, the agency must notify them as soon as possible that they cannot be considered suitable to adopt a child.

Confidentiality of CRB disclosures

Where the application is made by a couple, the agency should only inform the applicant who is the convicted or cautioned individual of the specific reason for terminating the application. Guidance requires that the assessing social worker should "explain to that person that the agency may not inform the other person of the conviction or caution but will inform them that as a consequence of information obtained from the checks the joint application cannot proceed."

In advising the person with the conviction or caution, "the agency may consider it appropriate to suggest that they consider disclosing their conviction or caution to the other person so that that person has a clear understanding of why the joint application cannot proceed."

Where the checks lead to the agency obtaining information about another adult member of the household being convicted or cautioned for a specified offence, the agency is again restricted from disclosing this to anyone. It may inform other adult household members and suggest that they inform the applicants, but it may not do so itself. In such a case, the agency should counsel the applicants that its checks indicate that the agency should not proceed with their application.

Criminal offences which are not specified

If the CRB certificate reveals offences which are not specified and so do not prohibit the assessment from going any further, they may still be relevant to suitability. An obvious example is several recent drunk driving or public disorder offences which suggest the applicant has a serious alcohol problem.

Preparation for adoption

AAR 2005, 24 requires the agency to arrange for all prospective adopters to be given preparation for adoption. Some prospective adopters may already have recent experience of caring for a child, as parents, foster carers or child minders. Some may be applying to adopt for a second time. The agency should decide the nature of the preparation that is most appropriate for the prospective adopters. Preparation may be provided either by the agency itself or by arrangement with another agency or adoption support agency. AAR 2005, 24 stipulates that adoption preparation includes providing information to the prospective adopters about:

a) the age range, sex, likely needs and background of children who may be placed for adoption by the agency.
b) the significance of adoption for a child and their family.
c) contact between a child and their parent/guardian/other relatives.
d) the skills which are necessary for an adoptive parent.
e) the agency's procedures in relation to the assessment of prospective adopters and the placement of a child for adoption, and the application for the adoption order.

This preparation must include written information about the legal consequences and effects of adoption for the adopters and children.

Information gathering about prospective adopters

Agencies are required to obtain a wide range of information about prospective adopters (AAR 2005, 25.2). This information is set out in Schedule 4 Part 1 of AAR 2005 (reproduced in Appendix 2). Gathering this information and analysing it is part of the assessment process.

Medicals

The agency must obtain a written report from a registered medical practitioner about the health of prospective adopters, following a full examination, and the report must include the matters specified in the schedule (Appendix 2) unless the agency has been told by its medical adviser that such an examination and report is unnecessary (AAR 2005, 25.3 and Schedule 4 Part 2). This might be, for example, where the prospective adopters are foster carers and the agency already has their health report. A summary of the medical report is contained within the prospective adopters' report (see below) and so is made known to them. The content of the full health report is not usually disclosed to the prospective adopters, although they can ask the doctor who completed the report to disclose it to them.

Personal references

An agency must interview the persons nominated by the prospective adopters to provide personal references, and prepare a written report of these interviews (AAR 2005, 25.3.b). A minimum of three people must give personal references on the prospective adopters, only one of whom may be a relative. Some agencies may ask for more. The content of these interviews must not be disclosed by the agency to the prospective adopters unless the referees explicitly consent.

Enquiries of the applicants' local authority

AAR 2005 25.4 stipulates that the agency must ascertain whether the local authority in whose area the prospective adopters live has any information about them that may be relevant to the assessment, for example, any involvement on child protection matters. If so, the agency must obtain a written report from that authority.

Past relationships and parenting experiences

The information required includes "details of any experience the prospective adopter has had of caring for children (including as a parent, stepparent, foster parent, child minder or prospective adopter) and an assessment of their ability in this respect." (AAR 2005, 25)

Whilst it is not a legal requirement that the previous partners of prospective adopters (or their adult children) be approached by the agency as part of the investigation into their suitability, practice guidance from the DfES suggests that this is necessary and appropriate when the prospective adopters and their previous partners have parented children together, or the previous relationship has been lengthy or significant in the prospective adopter's life. An agency may not wish to proceed with an assessment if a prospective adopter is unwilling to agree to this, or to provide the information which will make this possible.

Determining the suitability of a couple to adopt

SAR 2005, 4.2 requires that "proper regard" is had by the agency and panel to the need for stability and permanence in their relationship. This requirement applies whether the couple are of different genders or the same gender, married or have entered into a civil partnership, or living together as partners in an enduring family relationship.

The Prospective Adopters Report (Form F)

At the end of the assessment, the agency social worker will prepare this report. It is presented to the adoption panel which will consider whether to recommend that the prospective adopters be approved as suitable to adopt a child (AAR 2005, 25.5). It includes the information about the prospective adopters and their family specified in Schedule 4, Part 1 (Appendix 2) and:

a) a summary, written by the agency's medical adviser, of the state of health of the prospective adopters.

b) any relevant information the agency obtains from the prospective adopters' local authority.

c) any observations stemming from information giving, preparation and counselling of the prospective adopters.

d) the agency's assessment of the prospective adopters' suitability to adopt a child and any other information which the agency considers to be relevant.

Initial draft and second opinion visit

The social worker who assesses the prospective adopter should draft the report for the adoption panel, highlighting any issues of concern, and submit it to their team manager. Where there are any issues of concern or clarification is needed, arrangements should be made for the team manager or another adoption social worker to visit the prospective adopters. The visit by another social worker provides the opportunity for securing a second opinion on the prospective adopters and their assessment before the report to the panel is finalised.

Brief Prospective Adopters Report – when an assessment is not completed

AAR 2005, 25.7 covers cases where before the agency's assessment is complete, information is revealed which leads the agency to consider that the prospective adopters may not be suitable to adopt.

The agency social worker must prepare a Brief Prospective Adopters Report and should seek advice from their line manager and, as appropriate, the agency's medical or legal adviser. The agency should counsel the prospective adopters, involving these other professionals as appropriate. As a result of this counselling and advice, the prospective adopters may decide to withdraw their application. If the prospective adopters do not withdraw, the agency must present the brief Prospective Adopters Report to the adoption panel.

Prospective adopters' views on the report

When a Prospective Adopters Report or Brief Prospective Adopters Report is completed, the prospective adopters must be sent a copy of it, and have 10 working days opportunity to comment before the panel meeting (AAR 2005, 26).

Referral to the adoption panel

The agency must then send the Prospective Adopters Report or brief report to the adoption panel with the prospective adopters' views. It must also send a summary of the health report on the prospective adopters, the report on the interviews with personal referees, and where relevant the report from the prospective adopters' local authority. (The two latter reports are not shared with the prospective adopters.) AAR 2005, 25.10 obliges the agency to obtain any further information required by the panel, so far as is reasonably practicable.

Recommending approval

The panel must consider the Prospective Adopters Report or brief report and any other information, and make a recommendation to the agency as to whether the prospective adopters are suitable to adopt a child. (AAR 2005, 26)

The range of approval

An agency's decision that applicants are suitable to adopt is not conditional upon the range of children (age, gender number etc) that they might be considered suitable to adopt.

AAR 2005, 26.3 allows the panel to consider and advise the agency about the number of children the prospective adopters may be suitable to adopt, their age range, gender, likely needs and background. However the agency and prospective adopters are not restricted by such advice – it is not a formal recommendation, and the agency is not required to seek panel approval to place children whose characteristics do not comply with that advice. Prospective adopters should however be told of the panel's advice and keep it in mind when considering children offered to them.

Some adoption agencies, on medical advice, operate a policy in respect of adopters who smoke. For example, children under three years old, or who had or currently have respiratory conditions, will not be placed with them. Prospective adopters should be made aware of this policy during their preparation and assessment.

Prospective adopters attending panel

AAR 2005, 26.4 states that the panel must invite prospective adopters to attend the panel meeting considering their assessment before it makes a recommendation about their suitability to adopt. The agency should make it clear to the prospective adopters that the meeting is to provide an opportunity to discuss and clarify their reasons for wishing to adopt, and any other matters considered relevant to the application by the panel or the prospective adopters. It is not part of their assessment. Attendance at panel is not obligatory, and if prospective adopters decline the invitation that must not be a reason for recommending that they are unsuitable to adopt.

Agency decision

When the agency receives the recommendation of the adoption panel, the agency decision maker (a senior officer) must decide whether the prospective adopters are suitable to adopt a child, taking into consideration the minutes of the panel meeting, the reports submitted to the panel and concerns (if any) that are recorded in the minutes. The agency decision maker's decision, the reasons for it, and any views the decision maker has on the panel's advice, should be recorded on the prospective adopters' case record (AAR 2005, 27).

The agency's decision should be taken within seven working days of the adoption panel's recommendation (in Wales this should be as soon as possible). The prospective adopters should be informed orally of the agency's decision within two working days and written confirmation should be sent to them within five working days.

Where the decision maker decides not to accept the adoption panel recommendation, they should discuss this with another senior person in the agency who is not a panel member. The outcome of that discussion should be recorded on the prospective adopters' case record. Members of the panel cannot take part in the agency's decision.

Where the agency decides to approve the prospective adopters as suitable to adopt a child, it must notify them in writing. This letter confirming approval should inform the prospective adopters whether and how the panel advised about the age range, gender and number of children the prospective adopters would be most suitable for.

Where the agency considers that the prospective adopters are not suitable to adopt a child, AAR 2005 27.4 requires the agency to notify the prospective adopters in writing that it proposes not to approve them - this is a 'qualifying determination'. The agency must send its reasons with the notification to the prospective adopters, together with a copy of the recommendation of the adoption panel if that recommendation is different from the qualifying determination.

The Independent Review Mechanism (IRM)

The agency must also advise prospective adopters whom they propose not to approve or to terminate their approval (a 'qualifying determination') that within 40 working days, they may either submit representations to the agency, or apply for a review of the qualifying determination by an independent review panel (in Wales this period is 20 days). This review is free of charge to adoptive applicants. There is a charge to the agency of over £2000. In England the IRM is operated by the British Association for Adoption and Fostering. The Welsh equivalent is run by the Welsh Assembly and operates in respect of qualifying determinations made after 1 April 2006.

Where the prospective adopters do not make any representations to the agency or apply for a review by the IRM within 40 working days, the agency can proceed to make its decision and notify the prospective adopters in writing together with the reasons for that decision.

Where the agency receives further representations from the prospective adopters within 40 working days, it may refer the case, together with all the relevant information, to the adoption panel for further consideration. It is not, however, obliged to do so.

Where the agency refers the case to the panel, it has to consider the case again and make a fresh recommendation to the agency as to whether the prospective adopters are suitable to adopt a child.

Where the agency refers the case back to the agency panel or where the prospective adopters apply for a review by an IRM panel, the agency can only make the decision after taking into account the recommendations of the adoption panel, or the IRM panel.

The IRM panel can recommend approval, or concur with the agency that the applicants should not be approved. In the case of a brief prospective adopters report, the IRM panel can recommend that the assessment by the agency is continued or not continued. The panel does not have the power to overturn the agency's proposal – it is a review not an appeal – and the subsequent agency decision is final. Nonetheless, the first two years of operation of the IRM (up to 29 April 2006), suggests that the independent review panels are having a substantial impact, as a powerful second opinion, upon some adoption agencies decision making.

Reviews of approved adopters

AAR 2005, 29 requires an agency to review the prospective adopters' approval periodically until a child is placed for adoption. A review should take place whenever the agency considers it necessary, but otherwise yearly after approval (in Wales this is every two years). When carrying out a review, the agency must make enquiries and obtain any information it considers necessary in order to consider whether the prospective adopters continue to be suitable to adopt, and ascertain and take into account the prospective adopters' views.

The social worker conducting the review should be the adoption team manager or a social worker who did not conduct the original assessment. The review should consider the prospective adopters' family circumstances, health, economic circumstances, work commitments, and whether police and medical checks are still current. Guidance suggests that if CRB checks are more than two years old, they should be renewed. The prospective adopters should be asked whether their health remains unchanged, and the agency may take advice on whether health reports should be updated. Where the agency completes its review and considers that the prospective adopters remain suitable to adopt, it should inform the prospective adopters and note it on their case record.

Termination of approval

An adoption agency may consider that prospective adopters are no longer suitable to adopt after a 'routine' review, but also where the placement of a child has disrupted, or new information is received about, for example, illness or disability. In cases like this, the agency must undertake a review of the prospective adopters' approval.

Prospective Adopters Review Report

Where an agency thinks the prospective adopters are no longer suitable to adopt, it must prepare a written report that includes their reasons, notify the prospective adopters that their case is to be referred to the adoption panel, and give them a copy of the report, with 10 working days opportunity to send any views on it to the agency before panel meets. After the panel makes a recommendation the agency must decide what it proposes to do.

An agency proposal to terminate approval is a 'qualifying determination', entitling the prospective adopters to request a review by the IRM. The IRM panel can recommend that the approval continues or concur with the agency that it should not. Again the IRM panel does not have the power to overturn the agency's proposal – it is a review, and the subsequent agency decision is final.

Prospective intercountry adopters

'Intercountry adoption' is a general term referring to the adoption of a child resident abroad by people resident in the United Kingdom; it may also refer to the adoption of a child resident in the United Kingdom by people resident overseas. After ratification of the 1993 Hague Convention on Protection of Children and Cooperation in Respect of Intercountry Adoption the UK is part of an international system of collaboration that aims to prevent the abduction of, sale of, or trafficking in children.

UK residents may adopt children from overseas subject to compliance with intercountry adoption law. For example, it is a criminal offence for anyone habitually resident in the British Islands, other than a parent or guardian, to bring a child into the UK for adoption unless they are legally eligible to adopt in the UK, and they comply with all the regulations. These include that:
1. they must have been assessed and approved by a local authority or registered adoption agency in the UK, in accordance with the Adoption Agencies Regulations 2005 (in a very similar way to domestic agency adopters).
2. their approval must have been endorsed by the Secretary of State.
3. except where an overseas adoption order has been made or is to be made, the adopters must tell their local authority within 14 days of the child's arrival into the UK if they intend to apply for an adoption order or intend not to continue to give a home to the child.

Taking children out of the UK for adoption
It is a criminal offence to remove a child who is habitually resident in the UK for the purposes of adoption, except by a parent, relative or guardian, unless the prospective adopters have complied with

regulations, including an assessment of their suitability, and
have been granted an order (ACA 2002, Section 84) giving them
parental responsibility for the child. Expert legal advice will be
required. Intercountry adoption law is set out in ACA 2002, Adoption
(Intercountry Aspects) Act 1999, and the Adoptions with a Foreign
Element Regulations 2005.

Implications for agency adopters

The regulations and statutory guidance described in this chapter,
together with the inspection and registration regimes for agencies
described in chapter 1, are intended to ensure that prospective
adopters are treated fairly, openly and without discrimination in
the assessment and approval process. Transparency and openness
is encouraged by the requirement that prospective adopters see
and have 10 working days opportunity to comment on reports
about them going to panel. They therefore know the results of their
assessment and what the panel is being told about them. They also
have the chance to speak to the adoption panel directly.

The Independent Review Mechanism was set up to address
inconsistency and unfairness by some agencies in the assessment,
approval and review process for prospective adopters, and provides
those whom an agency proposes not to approve, or to terminate
their approval, with access to an independent consideration of the
agency's decision making.

However, no system is perfect, and some people going through
the assessment and approval process may yet have unhappy or
unjust experiences. Chapter 9 sets out ways to remedy problems
and achieve redress, if how they been treated is not in compliance
with the law, regulations and guidance or Human Rights. Whilst
the Human Right to a fair hearing (Article 6) informs how adoption
agencies approach their decision making, there is no Human
Right to create a family by adoption, or even to be assessed. The
Human Right not to be discriminated against is qualified by the
need to have regard when making decisions about a prospective
adopter's suitability, and to the right of a child to a safe, stable and
loving family life. The welfare of a child is always the paramount
consideration for adoption agencies and courts.

Children and adoption

This chapter sets out the legal requirements for adoption agencies in gathering information about and planning adoption for children, the legal circumstances of children involved in adoption and the implications for their prospective adopters.

The meaning of the terms parental responsibility, parent, guardian, residence order and special guardianship order are explained in the introduction to this book.

The welfare of the child

The Children Act 1989 and the Adoption and Children Act 2002 both require that the welfare of children is paramount when courts or agencies are making decisions, including decisions about adoption. Courts are also required to timetable care, placement and adoption proceedings as quickly as possible, (unless it is not appropriate) because delays in decision making are likely to have a negative impact on the child's welfare.
Another important principle when courts are considering applications is that no order should be made unless it's better for the child than not doing so. In other words - is the order applied for the one which will best protect and promote the child's welfare, or should a different order be made, or no order at all?

Welfare checklist for children (ACA 2002, Section 1 (4))

When making decisions about placement for adoption, courts and agencies must take into account:
a) the child's ascertainable wishes and feelings regarding the decision (in the light of the child's age and understanding).
b) the child's particular needs.

c) the likely effect on the child (throughout their life) of having ceased to be a member of the original family and become an adopted person.

d) the child's age, sex, background and any of the child's characteristics which the court or agency considers relevant.

e) any harm which the child has suffered or is at risk of suffering.

f) the relationship the child has with relatives, and with any other person in relation to whom the court or agency considers the relationship to be relevant (Section 1 (4) f)). This includes;

i) the likelihood of any such relationship continuing and the value to the child of its doing so.

ii) the ability and willingness of any of the child's relatives, or any such person, to provide the child with a secure environment in which the child can develop, and otherwise meet the child's needs.

iii) the wishes and feelings of the child's relatives or any such person, regarding the child.

Implications for adopters

The welfare of children as paramount means that all decision making by agencies and courts should have the welfare of children at its core – more important than the interests or welfare of parents, relatives, foster carers or adopters. This sounds like an easy principle to follow, but in practice it is not, due to the competing and sometimes heart-wrenching calls of other people for their wishes and feelings and rights to be taken into account.

The importance of birth relatives to children involved in adoption is recognised in Section 1 (4) (f) above, and its inclusion in the welfare checklist is designed to ensure that a child's relationships with birth parents and other people in the past and present are not dismissed as insignificant to their future. This section is of particular relevance to contact issues (see chapter 6).

Non-agency adoptions

Children being adopted by their stepparents, relatives, or private foster carers may be subject to court orders under the Children Act 1989 – such as residence. contact, special guardianship, or interim care orders and care orders, or no orders.

The type of order (if any) and to whom it has been granted, will determine who has parental responsibility for the child, with whom it is shared, who may have contact with the child, and whose consent to the making of an adoption order must be given or dispensed with by a court. Prospective adopters of a child brought into the UK from abroad may or may not be the subject of an order made in their country of origin. The nature of the order will determine if the consent of parents and guardians to the making of an adoption order has been given or will need to be dispensed with by a court.

Looked after children living with local authority foster carers might be the subject of applications by their foster carers to adopt them without the support of the local authority. These are non-agency adoptions. These children will be either accommodated (Children Act 1989, Section 20), in which case only parents and guardians have parental responsibility, or subject to care orders or placement orders, when parental responsibility is shared between parents and guardians, and the local authority.

However, having parental responsibility for a child does not allow the parent, guardian or local authority to prevent an application for an adoption order being made, and the application has the legal effect of preventing the removal of the child from the prospective adopters until and unless leave of court is given, or there are child protection concerns. Applications cannot be made until a child has lived with non-agency adopters for specified periods of time – ranging from six months to three years – and making the application for an adoption order does not guarantee that the order will be made (see chapter 8).

Local authority duties towards children in non-agency adoptions

Where non-agency prospective adopters give notice to a local authority of their intention to apply for an adoption order (ACA 2002, Section 44 - see chapter 8), they must allow a social worker from the local authority "sufficient opportunities to see the child with the applicants (both if they are a couple) in the home environment". The social worker must investigate the suitability of the proposed adopters, and whether the application is in the best interests of the child, before preparing a court report.

Agency adoptions

An adoption agency must refer cases of looked after children for whom adoption is being considered to their adoption panel, for a recommendation that the child "should be placed for adoption". After taking that recommendation into account, the agency must make a decision.

Timescales for adoption planning for looked after children

Adoption Guidance (statutory) requires that these timescales should generally be adhered to unless the agency considers that in a particular case it would not be in the child's interests – the paramount consideration must always be the welfare of the child. Where the agency is unable to comply with a timescale or decides not to, it should record the reasons on the child's case record.

The child's need for a permanent home should be addressed and a plan to achieve it made by the time of the statutory review held four months after a child has first become looked after. Often a permanence plan will be made much earlier than this, within a few weeks of the child becoming looked after. At this stage it will probably be a 'parallel' or 'twin track' plan – to explore several different routes to permanence at the same time, e.g. return home, care by relatives, as well as adoption whilst assessments of the child and parents and possibly other family members are undertaken.

The adoption panel's recommendation as to whether the child should be placed for adoption must be made within two months of a statutory review which endorses the local authority's view (after all assessments are completed) that adoption is the permanence plan. In other words, the child's local authority has finished 'twin track' or 'parallel' planning and concluded that other options for permanence like return home, kinship care or fostering, are ruled out as not in the child's best interests.

The agency's decision on whether the child should be placed for adoption should be taken within seven working days of the adoption panel's recommendation.

Child's Permanence Report (in Wales the Child's Adoption Assessment Report)

This new report is a legal requirement under the Adoption Agencies Regulation 2005. As part of the Integrated Children's System operated by local authorities, a child's social worker will start compiling this comprehensive report on a child when they first become looked after by the local authority, and continue to do so as long as the child remains looked after. It is a crucial part of permanence planning for a child, whatever that plan is. Where adoption is being considered for a child the Child's Permanence Report must be presented to the panel when it is asked to make a recommendation as to whether the child should be placed for adoption (AAR 2005, 17).

The content of the Child's Permanence Report is set out in Appendix 3. It is a vital document for prospective adopters as it is also the report which they will be given when they are first approached about a proposed placement of a child (see chapter 4).

Legal circumstances of babies relinquished for adoption under six weeks of age

A birth mother is not regarded as legally competent to give her formal consent to her baby's placement for adoption until her child is six weeks old. However, some mothers (and fathers) choose adoption for their baby prior to, or shortly after birth, and wish their child to be in the care of adopters as soon as possible. A mother (and father if they have parental responsibility) must agree in writing with the agency that their child be placed for adoption (AAR 2005, 35 (4)).

Birth father without parental responsibility

Where the identity of the birth father without parental responsibility is known to the adoption agency and the agency is satisfied it is appropriate to do so, the agency must inform, advise and counsel him and find out as far as is possible whether he intends to acquire parental responsibility for his child or a contact or residence order (AAR 2005, 14 (4)).

The extent to which the agency pursues these enquiries is a matter for its judgement, taking into account and balancing his wishes and

3

Human Rights with those of the mother, and the child's Human Rights, needs and welfare. Amongst other things, the agency will have to consider the delays that these enquiries may cause in achieving the mother's choice of placement with adopters for her child as soon as possible after birth.

Before making the placement

Whilst prospective adopters may have been told of a possible placement before or soon after the birth, the placement cannot happen until the agreement with the parents has been signed and the requirements of AAR 2005, 11-33 have been carried out:

1. The agency provides information, counselling and advice to the parents as far as possible, and considered appropriate, including about the legal implications.
2. The agency completes the Child's Permanence Report including medical information about the child and birth family.
3. The agency completes the Adoption Placement Report in consultation with the prospetive adopters.
4. The child's case is referred to the adoption panel for recommendation that the child should be placed for adoption, and the match with particular prospective adopters.
5. The agency makes those decisions. and prepares an Adoption Placement Plan (see chapter 4) in consultation with the prospective adopters.
6. The prospective adopters are content with the placement plan, and agree to proceed.

Legal consequences of placement under six weeks by agreement

The parents or guardians retain parental responsibility and no one else has it. However there are restrictions on their entitlement to have contact with the child, or have them returned, if they change their minds.

If the parents do request their child's return, the adoption agency has seven days in which to return the child, or avoid that duty by applying for a placement order (see below). The prospective adopters will not be able to apply for an adoption order, (avoiding their legal obligation to give up the child), until the child has lived with them for at least 10 weeks.

Contact between the child and their parents is at the discretion of the adoption agency (taking into account the views of the prospective adopters, the parents and the welfare of the child), or parents or guardians will be able to apply for section 26 contact orders (see chapters 4 and 6).

When the child reaches six weeks old, and to avoid the legal duty to return the child at the request of the parents or guardians, the placement must be authorised by the giving of section 19 consent by the birth parents with parental responsibility and the guardians, or by granting a placement order. The prospective adopters may apply for an adoption order when the child has lived them for at least 10 weeks. When this application is with the court, neither the adoption agency nor the parents may remove the child unless the court gives leave (unless a local authority has child protection concerns).

Implications for prospective adopters

This legal provision for placing a child for adoption under six weeks old, described in a parliamentary debate in 2004 as the "fast track to adoption for babies", may not be attractive to adoption agencies or prospective adopters. There is an extremely tight timetable to achieve all the regulatory requirements within six weeks of birth, along with the risk of having to return the child if the parents change their minds about adoption.

However, if parents are unwavering about the choice of adoption for their child, there are obvious benefits for them, the prospective adopters and the child. Prospective adopters need, and are entitled to, expert advice and counselling about the risks and advantages of these placements.

Legal circumstances of children relinquished for adoption over six weeks of age

Authorising adoptive placement by parental consent (ACA 2002, Section 19)

An adoption agency may not place a relinquished child for adoption over six weeks of age unless placement has been legally authorised by parental consent, or a court grants a placement order.

Parents with parental responsibility and guardians relinquishing their child for adoption must give formal consent to placement under Section 19 of ACA 2002. The consent must be given in writing and witnessed by a CAFCASS officer (or officer of the Welsh Assembly), who must ensure that consent is given unconditionally and with full understanding.

Section 19 consent can be specific to a placement with particular adopters, or to any adopters chosen by the agency. A birth mother cannot give her Section 19 consent until her child is six weeks old. A father acquiring parental responsibility after the mother has consented and child has been placed for adoption is deemed to have also consented, although he may withdraw his deemed consent.

Where the identity of a birth father without parental responsibility is known to the adoption agency and it is satisfied it is appropriate to do so, the agency must inform, advise and counsel him and ascertain whether he intends to acquire either parental responsibility for his child or a contact or residence order. The extent to which the agency pursues these enquiries is a matter for its judgement, taking into account and balancing his wishes and Human Rights with those of the mother, and the child's Human Rights, needs and welfare.

The agency will have to consider the delays that these enquiries may cause in achieving a placement within the three month timescale required by statutory guidance for relinquished children under six months of age. Section 19 consent can be withdrawn at any time until the application for an adoption order is made.

Advance consent to making a future adoption order (ACA 2002, Section 20)

Parents and guardians can give advance consent to the making of an adoption order under Section 20, when giving Section 19 consent, or subsequently, and may also notify the adoption agency that they do not wish to be notified of the application for an adoption order. Section 20 consent and notice can be withdrawn, up to the application for an adoption order being made. If Section 20 consent and notice is not given, or is given and then withdrawn, the relinquishing parents or guardians must be notified of the time and court venue of the application for an adoption order (see chapter 8).

Legal consequences of giving Section 19 consent

The parents or guardians retain parental responsibility, shared with the adoption agency, and with the prospective adopters on placement.

The adoption agency decides the extent to which prospective adopters and parents can exercise parental responsibility (see chapter 4 - placement plans). There are restrictions on the parents' entitlement to have contact with their child, or to have them returned, if they withdraw their consent. If the parents do withdraw their consent and the child is not yet placed for adoption, the adoption agency has seven days to return the child, or avoid the duty to do so by applying for a placement order.

If parents withdraw their consent after the child has been placed for adoption, the prospective adopters must return the child to the agency and the agency must return the child to their parents within 14 days of the withdrawal notice, or avoid the duty to do so by applying for a placement order. The prospective adopters will not be able to apply for an adoption order (avoiding their obligation to return the child), until the child has lived with them for at least 10 weeks.

Neither the local authority nor the prospective adopters can cause the child to be known by a new surname, or remove them from the UK for more than one month, without leave of court or written permission of each parent or guardian.

Contact between the child and their parents will be at the discretion of the adoption agency who will take into account the views of the prospective adopters, the parents and the welfare of the child. Parents, guardians and some relatives will be able to apply for Section 26 contact orders (see chapters 4 and 6).

On application for an adoption order

The withdrawal of Section 19 consent (and Section 20 consent) has no legal effect after an adoption order has been applied for. If Section 19 or 20 consent has not been withdrawn before the adoption order is applied for the parents or guardians cannot oppose the making of an adoption order unless the court gives them permission ('leave' in legal terminology) (see chapter 8 for more detail).

Implications for adopters

Before an adoption agency can place a relinquished child over six weeks old with prospective adopters it must ask the adoption panel for a recommendation, and then decide that the child should be placed for adoption. As part of that decision making process the agency should consider if any alternative to adoption (e.g. a kinship placement) would better meet the child's needs. The parents or guardians, after advice and counselling, must consent to placement formally. This consent must be witnessed by a CAFCASS officer who has to ensure consent is given unconditionally and with full understanding of the legal consequences.

In these circumstances, most adoptive placements of relinquished children will turn out to be secure. However, they will be vulnerable, especially in the first 10 weeks of placement, to the possibility of the withdrawal of Section 19 consent.

Whilst an application for a placement order will avoid the duty to return a child at the parents' request, a court will not grant a placement order unless it agrees that the child should to be placed for adoption, and is at risk of suffering significant harm if returned to the parents. Although some relinquished children may have potentially abusive parents, most do not.

On the other hand, where parents consent and remain of the same view, in particular where they have consented to a placement with adopters they have had a part in choosing (perhaps from a description, rather than by knowing their identity), the goodwill between the parents and prospective adopters augurs well for the success of the placement, any plans for contact, and the emotional health of all concerned.

Contact

The Section 19 consent ends the local authority's legal duty to promote contact to the child, but parents, guardians and some relatives will be able to apply for contact orders before and during the adoptive placement (see chapters 4 and 6).

Parents and guardians retain parental responsibility for the child, although this will likely be severely restricted, and will be shared with the local authority, and with the prospective adopters on placement. The implications for prospective adopters sharing parental responsibility during placement are in chapters 4 and 7.

Retaining parental responsibility after giving Section 19 consent means that parents and guardians must be notified of the date and court venue for the application for an adoption order, and can seek leave to oppose it (unless they have given Section 20 notice – see above). Parents and guardians who have not asked for leave to oppose the adoption order are entitled to attend the hearing and be heard, as well as apply for contact orders to be made. Parents and guardians who have been refused leave to oppose cannot be heard on whether the adoption order should be granted, but can still attend court and apply for contact orders.

Legal circumstances of children placed for adoption without parental consent

Authorising placement for adoption

An adoption agency may not place a child over six weeks of age for adoption unless placement has been legally authorised by consent under section 19, or the granting of a placement order.

Children cannot be placed for adoption subject to care orders. Freeing for adoption orders were abolished on 30 December 2005, but freeing orders granted before then (or granted following an application made in 2005) continue in force until an adoption order is made or the freeing order revoked. If the freeing order is revoked any previous care order will reactivate.

Placement orders (ACA 2002, Section 21)

A placement order gives a local authority the legal entitlement to place a child for adoption with any adopters chosen by the agency. Placement orders must be granted before the children can be placed with prospective adopters.

The majority of children looked after by local authorities and in need of adoptive families will be the subject of ongoing care proceedings (a care order application) when a local authority applies for the placement order to authorise adoptive placement.

An adoption agency must refer cases of looked after children for whom adoption is being considered to their adoption panel, for a recommendation that the child be placed for adoption. After taking that recommendation into account, the agency must make a decision.

A local authority has a legal duty to apply for a placement order once it has decided a child should be placed for adoption. The application must be made within the care proceedings, when a care plan for adoption is formulated and submitted to the court, unless (unusually) Section 19 consent is given by parents and guardians.

A court will not grant a placement order unless it is satisfied that the child should be placed for adoption, and is suffering or at risk of suffering significant harm due to the standard of parental care. (The latter is the same 'threshold test' applied by a court as for a care order under Section 31, Children Act 1989).

Parents and guardians may consent to placement for adoption during the care or placement proceedings, but in most cases they will not. In these cases, the court is asked to dispense with their consent to placement on the grounds either that they cannot be found, or are incapable of consenting (e.g. because of disability or ill health), or the welfare of the child requires their consent to be dispensed with.

The legal consequences of a placement order

Granting a placement order has many important legal consequences:
1. When a placement order is granted any care order ceases to have legal effect. It is suspended, but not discharged, the child is still looked after, and the care order will 'reactivate' if the placement order is revoked.
2. When a placement order is granted and after placement with prospective adopters, a child can be removed from them by the local authority (until they apply for the adoption order), but cannot by removed by the parents or guardians.
3. The prospective adopters have parental responsibility for the child from placement, shared with the local authority and parents and guardians. However, the local authority decides the extent to which prospective adopters and parents or guardians can exercise that parental responsibility (see chapter 4 - placement plans).

4. Neither the local authority nor the prospective adopters can cause the child to be known by a new surname, or remove them from UK for more than one month without leave of court or written permission of each parent with parental responsibility or guardian.
5. Contact between a child and birth family is at the discretion of the local authority. Parents, guardians and some relatives can apply for Section 26 contact orders (see chapters 4 and 6).
6. No application to revoke a placement order can be made by parents or guardians once the child has been placed for adoption.

On the application for an adoption order

The application for an adoption order cannot be made by agency adopters until the child has lived with them for at least 10 weeks. When a child is subject to a placement order, and an application is made for an adoption order, the adopters do not need to ask the court to dispense with the parents or guardians' consent to the making of the adoption order, and the parents or guardians may not oppose the making of this order unless the court gives them leave (see chapter 8). The local authority may not remove the child from the adopters without the permission of the court (unless there are child protection concerns).

Implications for adopters

The majority of children placed with agency adopters will be subject to placement orders. Therefore before an adoptive placement can happen a court has decided that the child should be placed for adoption, and that they have suffered, or would be at risk of suffering, significant harm due to the standard of parental care. This decision will have been made following a court hearing where parents and guardians are legally represented, and a CAFCASS officer has advised the court on behalf of the child.

A court which has recently dispensed with the consent of parents or guardians on 'significant harm' grounds is unlikely to readily give them leave to oppose the making of an adoption order. Therefore the prospective adopters can be reasonably confident that their application for an adoption order will proceed without being contested by the parents or guardians - especially if the adoption order application is made before there has been much time for parents or guardians to effect a positive change in their circumstances since the placement order was made, to warrant leave to oppose being given.

The placement order ends the local authority's legal duty to promote contact to a looked after child, but parents, guardians and some relatives will be able to apply for contact orders before and during the adoptive placement (see chapters 4 and 6).

Parents and guardians will retain parental responsibility for the children, although it is likely to be severely restricted and will be shared with the local authority, and also with the prospective adopters on placement. The implications for prospective adopters having parental responsibility during placement are set out in chapters 4 and 7.

Retaining parental responsibility after a placement order is granted means that parents and guardians must be notified of the date and venue for the adoption order application, and can apply to the court for permission to oppose the making of the order. Even if not given leave to oppose, court rules allow any parent or guardian to be heard by the court about whether the adoption order should be made, unless a parent gave Section 20 consent and notice that they did not wish to be heard. Parents and guardians can also apply for Section 8 contact orders to be made with the adoption order.

Therefore there is small window of opportunity for parents and guardians to obtain leave to oppose the making of an adoption order, and to have contact orders made with adoption orders. A further discussion of the implications for prospective adopters at the application for an adoption order stage and in terms of contact, is in chapter 8. This also covers the criteria for leave to oppose being given.

3

The timing of placement orders and matching child and adoptive family – implications for adopters

A child over six weeks of age cannot be placed for adoption by an agency until a placement order has been granted (or Section 19 consent given). Once the agency has decided a child should be placed for adoption and whilst the application for a placement order is being considered by the court, local authorities will begin enquiries on their own and with other agencies via the local consortium or the Adoption Register to look for potential adoptive families for the child.

Regulations allow adoption agencies to approach approved adopters (with the Child's Permanence Report) when placement orders have been applied for, but not yet granted, to ascertain if they would be interested in adopting the child.

However, careful thought needs to be given to whether it is appropriate to do so at this stage, or whether the approach to prospective adopters and the panel meeting for matching child and family should wait until the placement order has been secured.

If approaches are made to prospective adopters, and/or matches between them and a child approved by agencies before the court has granted the placement order, the prospective adopters will have an anxious wait for the outcome of the court proceedings. These are at risk of postponement and delay, as well as the chance that the placement order is not granted, and the placement cannot proceed. It also opens the prospective adopters up to the possibility that the court and/or CAFCASS officer will want to make their own examination and judgement of the suitability of the adoptive family identified for the child, even though they have already been considered or approved as a suitable match by the agency.

Identifying the prospective adopters of a child by approaching and/or matching them with a child before the placement order is granted may have further problematic implications as the prospective adopters then become in law the people "with whom a child is to live". If applications are made for Section 26 contact

3

orders in the placement order proceedings (see chapters 4 and 6) they will be respondents (legal parties) to the court proceedings. This puts the prospective adopters in the position of needing legal representation in the placement order proceedings, because the court must hear their views about contact after placement, at a time when it is not certain that the agency will secure the legal authority to place the child with them.

Whilst it may be helpful to the court to know the prospective adopters' views in making decisions about Section 26 contact order applications, the prospective adopters are likely to be very troubled about being involved in court proceedings before the court has determined if the child can be placed for adoption at all, let alone with them. This may be extremely stressful for the prospective adopters and can easily be avoided by not approaching them until the placement order is granted.

However, there are some appropriate reasons for prospective adopters to be approached before the placement order is granted, for example where the agency agrees that the child's current foster carers should adopt them, or if the child is to be placed in an adoptive family who have already adopted the child's older siblings.

Apart from these exceptions, approved prospective adopters should be careful to ensure that the child's agency does not approach them about a child prematurely or inappropriately before a placement order is granted. If an approach is made before the placement order is granted, prospective adopters should ask for, and are entitled to have, separate legal advice funded by the child's agency, who should also meet their legal costs if they become respondents to Section 26 contact order applications.

3

Proposing, planning and making adoptive placements

This chapter sets out the legal obligations for adoption agencies to give information to prospective adopters about the children offered to them, and when and what information must be provided. It also covers the requirements that adoption agencies must comply with when proposing and approving matches between children and prospective adopters, planning placements, including arrangements for contact, and support, and the exercise of parental responsibility by the prospective adopters during placement. The new law and regulations provide welcome clarity about these issues.

Timescales for making placements

Statutory guidance requires that these timescales should be adhered to, unless a child's agency considers that in a particular case it would not be in the child's interests.

Relinquished children
Where a parent has consented to the placement of their child aged between six weeks and under six months, a proposed placement with suitable prospective adopters should be identified and approved by the adoption panel within three months of the agency deciding that the child should be placed for adoption.

Children placed without parental consent, or relinquished over six months of age
A proposed placement with a suitable prospective adopter should be identified and approved by the panel within six months of the agency deciding that the child should be placed for adoption. However, this timescale may be difficult to achieve for children who have not been relinquished (are to be adopted against the wishes of their parents). These children become the subject of care and placement order

proceedings, and they cannot legally be placed for adoption until authorised by the granting of placement orders. There may be a considerable delay between the agency decision that a child should be placed for adoption and the granting of a placement order.

Choosing placements

Having gathered information about a number of possible prospective adopters, and once the placement order is secured, the child's agency will begin the process of identifying which family is likely to be the most suitable. The agency will compare their potential to provide a stable and permanent family for the child, based on the Child's Permanence Report, the prospective adopter's report and any other relevant other information.

Therefore, it is possible that several potential adoptive families will receive the Child's Permanence Report (Appendix 3) and any other information the agency considers relevant or the prospective adopters request. Other information could include full reports rather than summaries of the child's health, education or special needs. Videos and more photographs of the child may also be helpful to the prospective adopters.

AAR 2005, 31 (1)(a) refers to "any further information to the prospective adopter as may be required." Where prospective adopters (and/or their social workers) identify the need for more information, they can ask for it to be provided by the child's agency. This could include, for example, their social worker reading the child's local authority file or reading the full medical reports about the child.

Confidentiality of information

The agency should ensure that the prospective adopters confirm in writing that they will keep the information provided to them confidential, and that they will return it if the agency requests it (which they would, if their family is not chosen for that child).

Only one family to matching panel

Having made a choice of the family which the child's agency considers the most likely to be suitable, and confirmed that the prospective adopters are willing to proceed, the child's agency should present this one adoptive family to the panel for a proposed match.

Meeting about the proposed placement

The child's social worker must meet the prospective adopters to discuss the proposed placement and ascertain their views, including those on the agency's contact proposals for the child.

Planning support services for children to be placed for adoption

AAR 2005, 31 (2)(a) requires local authorities to undertake an assessment of adoption support service needs of the child, the adoptive parents and any child of the prospective adopters, when they are considering placing a child with particular adoptive families.

Implications for adopters

Prospective adopters receiving the news that an agency is considering a child for them and receiving information about that child, will be happy and excited. However, they need to retain some degree of 'hard headedness', to be able to analyse the information in terms of the possible impact on them - both the good and the less positive. When analysing the information they have received, they are advised to consult their social worker.

Their social worker will look at the information objectively, and in preparation for the first meeting with the child's social worker lead the prospective adopters towards thinking about particular issues – especially the type of support services they might need, and the proposed contact arrangements during placement or after adoption. At this first meeting with the child's social worker, the prospective adopters' agenda might include:

1. A request for any information which is not supplied (or is supplied, but is out of date or inadequate), or needs clarification.
2. Discussion of the proposed contact arrangements, including if and how it is proposed that they might alter after placement or adoption, (for example in response to a child's reaction or changing needs).
3. What support is to be built into the placement at the beginning, or is anticipated as being needed at a later point. (Support services are set out in chapter 5).

4

Explaining placement procedures

Prospective adopters should have received a general explanation of placement procedures as part of their initial preparation for assessment but the agency should now remind them of its placement planning procedures.

Where the prospective adopters were approved by one agency but the child is from another, they should receive an explanation of the introduction and placement procedures used by the child's agency.

Assessing the need for support services before placement

When the child's agency and the prospective adopters and their agency agree that the proposed placement should proceed, the child's local authority must assess the support needs of the adoptive family, including the child and the prospective adopters, and any other children of the prospective adopters.

Consideration must also be given to appropriate arrangements for contact with the child by the birth family or significant others.

Formulating the Adoption Placement Report

4

The child's social worker should provide the prospective adopters with a draft of the Adoption Placement Report (see below) and must meet them to discuss the proposed placement, and ascertain their views, including their views on the agency's proposals for allowing any person contact with the child. This report must be prepared by a social worker who is suitably qualified and experienced in child care and adoption work or supervised by a suitably qualified social worker, who must approve the report.

The Adoption Placement Report

After meetings and discussions based around the draft Adoption Placement Report, and at least 10 working days before the proposed match between the adoptive family and the child is presented to panel, the child's local authority must prepare and give the prospective adopters the final version of the Adoption Placement Report which includes:

1. The agency's reasons for proposing this placement (i.e. why this family for this child).
2. The prospective adopters' views about the proposed placement.

3. The proposals for contact.
4. The local authority's proposals for the provision of adoption support services for the adoptive family.
5. Any other information the agency considers relevant. This might, for example, include the views of the child about the proposed placement.

This report must be prepared by a social worker who is suitably qualified and experienced in child care and adoption work or supervised by a suitably qualified social worker, who must approve the report.

Prospective adopters' views
At least 10 working days before the adoption panel matching meeting the child's agency should invite the prospective adopters to submit their views on the Adoption Placement Report.

Implications for adopters

These are important new legal requirements; for full information about a child to be given to prospective adopters at a very early stage, for consultation with the adoptive family, for assessment of support needs and a written Adoption Placement Report upon which the adoptive family can comment. They provide significant safeguards for adopters and children. There should be no doubt as to what is proposed and has been agreed before the adoption panel recommends the placement, and the child's agency makes its decision.

It is important that prospective adopters don't, in their anxiety to progress the placement, agree to contact arrangements which, after careful consideration, and bearing in mind the needs and views of the child, they are unlikely to be comfortable with in the short or longer term. Similarly, prospective adopters should not be rushed in the assessment of their support needs.

Parental responsibility during adoptive placement
One issue not included in the Adoption Placement Report, but of considerable significance to prospective adopters, is the extent to which the child's local authority proposes to delegate the exercise of parental responsibility to them during the placement.

4

In the light of the information about the child, and therefore with some knowledge of what the important decisions about the child might be, (for example education or medical treatment), prospective adopters should be thinking about which decisions they would like to have delegated to them from the beginning of placement, and which they might wish to take on at a later stage.

The child's social worker will also need to consider this, and there may be agency policies about the delegation of parental responsibility to prospective adopters. Any policies should be applied with flexibility to proposed placements, taking into account the characteristics of the particular child and prospective adopters. For example, prospective adopters who are educational or medical professionals may be well placed and comfortable with making decisions about these matters sooner than others.

Settling-in grant

At this early point in moving towards a placement, prospective adopters might think about whether they are likely to need any financial help towards the purchase of furniture, or other equipment – car seats, a bigger car for a sibling group etc, or expenses for introductory visits to a child. The ASSR 2005 allows local authorities to provide financial help in these cases, and prospective adopters must not be means tested for this help as they are likely to be for other financial support. For very large settling-in expenses such as an extension or adaptation of a house, the prospective adopters may be means tested if they are paid financial support to purchase it. However, if the local authority provides the adaptation or extension by paying the builder or other supplier directly, it must not means test the prospective adopters.
It would be wise not to make any large financial commitments before the placement has been approved, and the proposed financial support is clear. Prospective adopters should also discuss with the child's social worker the extent of help that the child's local authority might provide for settling-in expenses. Chapter 6 describes financial support in more detail.

The adoption panel recommendation

After 10 working days, or earlier if the agency receives the prospective adopters' views sooner, the agency must send the adoption panel:

a) The Adoption Placement Report and the prospective adopter's views on that report.

b) The Child's Permanence Report

c) The Prospective Adopter's Report.

d) Any other relevant information requested by panel.

The adoption panel must consider the proposed placement and make a recommendation to the agency as to whether the child should be placed for adoption with that particular prospective adoptive family (AAR 2005, 32).

The panel must consider and may give advice to the agency about:

1. The proposals for providing adoption support services for the adoptive family.

2. The proposals for contact arrangements.

3. Whether the parental responsibility of the prospective adopters, and of the parents or guardians, should be restricted and, if so, to what extent.

The agency decision

The agency must take into account the panel's recommendation when deciding whether the child should be placed for adoption with the particular prospective adopters (AAR 2005, 33). Where the panel has provided the agency with advice, (about support, contact and exercise of parental responsibility) the decision maker may express a view on this advice.

The agency decision maker should consider the minutes of the panel meeting and the reports submitted to the panel. Where the decision maker is inclined to reject the adoption panel's recommendation, they should discuss this with another senior person in the agency who is not a panel member.

As soon as possible after making its decision, the agency is required to notify the prospective adopters in writing of the decision and, in an appropriate manner and taking into account the child's age and understanding, explain the decision to the child (AAR 2005, 33).

Placement planning meeting

Statutory guidance requires that after the agency decision to place a child with a particular family, the details of the placement should be planned at a meeting.

The agency should arrange for the prospective adopters and their social worker, the child's social worker, the child's current carer, and any relevant child specialists to attend the meeting. Statutory guidance suggests it may be helpful and appropriate to involve the foster carers' social worker.

The Adoption Placement Plan

As soon as possible after the placement planning meeting and before placement (in Wales this period must be at least seven days before placement), the child's agency must send the prospective adopters the Adoption Placement Plan. AAR 2005, Schedule 5 sets out the required content of this plan, including:

1. Whether the child is to be placed under a placement order or with the consent of the parent or guardian (see chapter 3 - The legal circumstances of the child).
2. The arrangements for preparing the child and the prospective adopters for the placement.
3. The proposed date for placing the child for adoption with the prospective adopters.
4. The arrangements for reviewing the placement (see chapter 7).
5. Whether the parental responsibility of the prospective adopters is to be restricted, and if so, to what extent (discussed above and below).
6. Where the local authority has decided to provide adoption support services for the adoptive family, how these will be provided and by whom (support services are discussed in chapter 5).
7. The arrangements that the adoption agency has made for allowing any person contact with the child, the form of contact, any Section

26 orders for contact, the arrangements for supporting contact, and the name and contact details of the person responsible for facilitating the contact arrangements (if applicable).

8. The dates when the child's life story book and later life letter are to be passed by the adoption agency to the prospective adopters.
9. Details of any other arrangements that need to be made.
10. The out of hours contact details for the child's and prospective adopter's social workers.

Implications for adopters

Exercise of parental responsibility

Statutory guidance and the wording of AAR 2005, 35(2) and schedule 5, "whether the parental responsibility of the prospective is to be restricted, and if so, the extent to which it is to be restricted" implies that the normal rule will be to delegate most decisions about the child to the prospective adopters during placement.

However, statutory guidance goes on to say "in some cases, the agency may consider it appropriate to retain some elements of parental responsibility when a child is placed, passing these to the prospective adopter as their parenting skills develop, for example:
1. Attendance at meetings and involvement in decisions about the child's special needs education.
2. Attendance at meetings and involvement in decisions about the child's CAMHS (Child and Adolescent Mental Heath Services) or other therapy.
3. Holidays and school trips overseas.
4. Choice of school, particularly where the child has special educational or other special needs."

The scheme of delegation or restriction of exercise of parental responsibility will need to be tailor-made to each placement and, as suggested above, any agency policies need to be applied flexibly to take account of individual circumstances, the views of the prospective adopters, the needs of the child and, if they are of sufficient understanding, the child's views.

4

Change of surname or taking the child out of the UK

There are two decisions which neither the child's agency nor the prospective adopters may take during placement even though they have shared parental responsibility:

1. Cause a child to be known by a new surname.
2. Take the child out of the UK for more than one month.

Both need the permission of a court, or the written permission of each parent or guardian with parental responsibility. Therefore a child cannot be registered at a school or doctor's surgery by the prospective adopters' surname when they are placed, unless the court has given permission for the child to be known by a new surname, or the parents or guardians have agreed to it. The latter is unlikely if they have opposed the making of the placement order.

Some children have surnames which might readily identify their origins or lead to their location becoming easily known after adoptive placement, names which are culturally problematic, and so on. In these circumstances prospective adopters might ask for an application to be made to the court for permission to cause the child to be known by the adopter's surname from placement. This might delay the placement but will protect the child and their adopters. The child's agency could anticipate and avoid any delay by asking for this permission in principle when the placement order is applied for, i.e. before the child is matched with prospective adopters.

Change of forename

Some children have forenames which they do not like, or might expose them to ridicule, or which are culturally problematic etc. The law does not expressly prohibit a change of forename for a child during an adoptive placement. In 2002 under the previous law, a High Court Judge ruled against a change of forename during adoptive placement as being a possible contravention of a child's Human Rights, because the prospective adopters did not have the legal entitlement to do so, and "to change a child's name is to take a significant step in a child's life. A child has names given to them by their parents. The child has a right to those names and retains that right. Those rights should not be set to one side, other than for good reasons."

This judgment might be regarded as slightly out of date, as it was given at a time when prospective adopters did not have parental responsibility during adoptive placement, and therefore had no legal entitlement to make any decisions about a child until the adoption order was granted. Under the new law the right to change a forename might be given to prospective adopters as part of the delegation of parental responsibility. In all cases the decision should be based on both an agreement between the child's agency and the prospective adopters (and the child if of sufficient understanding) as to what will best serve the child's interests and welfare, and in the words of the judgment above, for "good reasons" to change a forename.

Changing names after adoption

Adopters are entitled to change any part of a child's name on granting of the adoption order. They will be asked to give their chosen name for the child to the court when applying for the adoption order.

Other decisions during adoptive placement

Some decisions which could be delegated to prospective adopters, either on placement or later, and requiring careful thought, include:
a) Overnight stays (sleepovers) with friends or family. Should the prospective adopters or the child's agency give permission?
b) Holidays in the UK, or abroad, for less than one month.
c) Consent to routine medical or dental treatment of the child.
d) Decisions about a child's education.

Contact arrangements during placement

As suggested above, there needs to be careful consideration of which arrangements will best meet the child's needs, and which are acceptable to the prospective adopters. They also need to be considered in the light of any Section 26 contact orders that have been made with the placement order or might be applied for during the adoptive placement. Chapter 6 sets out how these arrangements or orders can be altered if the child's needs or other circumstances warrant a change, and any proposals for contact after the making of the adoption order.

In planning contact arrangements, prospective adopters must be frank about what is and is not likely to be acceptable to them. However they should also listen carefully to what is said about the child's needs, and with help from their social worker distinguish what is sometimes being put forward as a child's needs, but is actually about the needs of others (including themselves).

Support services
Prospective adopters also need to be frank, and well–informed, about what they might need as support services. Support services should be designed not just for the beginning of placement, but with the future in mind. For example, the need for therapy for attachment disorder may not emerge until a child's teenage years.

Prospective adopters' decision to proceed with the placement
AAR 2005, 35.3 provides that the agency may only place the child with the prospective adopters when the prospective adopters notify the agency that they wish to go ahead. The agency should keep the child's current carer informed of the placement arrangements and, bearing in mind the child's age and understanding, inform the child in an appropriate manner.

Child's medical and education records
AAR 2005, 35.6 requires the child's agency before the placement proceeds to:
1. Send to the prospective adopter's general practitioner written notification of the proposed placement, together with a report of the child's health history and current state of health.
2. Send written notification of the proposed placement to the local authority, if that authority is not the child's agency, and to the Primary Care Trust (England) or Local Health Board (Wales), for the area where the prospective adopter lives.
3. Where the child is of school age, send the local education authority for the area where the prospective adopter has their home, written notification of the proposed placement, information about the child's educational history and whether the child has been or is likely to be assessed for special educational needs.

Changes in the placement plan
AAR 2005, 35.7 requires the agency to notify the prospective adopter in writing of any change to the Adoption Placement Plan.

Support to adoptive families

Ensuring the right support to adopters of children from unhappy and abusive backgrounds is a cornerstone of the Government's reform of adoption law, and the first Adoption Support Regulations came into force in October 2003 – well before implementation of most of the new adoption law on 30 December 2005.

This chapter sets out the legal requirements under the Adoption Support Services Regulations for England and Wales (see Appendix 1), and statutory guidance. Together these cover the provision of adoption support services by local authorities and registered adoption support agencies, the range of those services, the role of the Adoption Support Services Adviser (ASSA) in local authorities, and the implications for adopters. ASSA refers to the Adoption Support Services Regulations 2005 (for England).

Duty to assess support needs

Local authorities have a legal duty to assess the support needs of adoptive families with whom they propose to place children, at any time during the adoptive placement, or after the adoption order, until the adopted person reaches 18 years old. Agency adoptive families have a legal right to this assessment, as and when they request it.

The timescale within which the assessment must be carried out is not specified in regulations or statutory guidance, but local authorities must act reasonably. A failure to provide an assessment within a reasonable time, especially if the need for support is urgent, and where the local authority has no reasonable excuse for the delay, can be challenged (see chapter 9). Claiming staff shortages as a reason not to undertake assessments is not acting reasonably.

There is a legal obligation for local authorities and other registered adoption support agencies to ensure that they have sufficient numbers of suitably qualified, competent and experienced persons working for their adoption service, to safeguard and promote the welfare of children receiving adoption support services.

Therefore, if a local authority lacks sufficient staff to undertake assessments or prepare adoption support plans, it is expected to commission the work from elsewhere, such as a suitably qualified and competent social worker, either independent or from a social work agency. Sometimes the assessment needs to be undertaken by someone with different skills, such as a therapist or psychologist assessing a child's need for specialist treatment. For example, if a local authority social worker (who is not a trained therapist) assesses a child whose adopters fear may need therapy, and the social worker believes the child's behaviour to be simply the result of adolescence, or the poor parenting skills of the adopters, the adopters may be able to challenge the assessment as being ill-founded because the social worker lacked the relevant qualifications.

Regulations require that a local authority must ensure that adoption support services provided to any person are appropriate having regard to the need for such services identified by an assessment carried out by the local authority.

Complaints about support

Complaints about assessment and support from the child's local authority must be made under their complaints procedures (see chapter 9). Adoption support agencies must establish a written procedure for considering complaints made by or on behalf of any person to whom the agency has provided or refused to provide support services.

The registered manager of an adoption support agency must ensure that any complaint made is fully investigated, and so far as is reasonably practicable, within 28 days of the complaint being received, inform the complainant of the outcome of the investigation and the action that is to be taken.

Assessment for adoption support services

Assessments are required to consider the following: the needs of the person being assessed and how these might be met; the needs of the adoptive family and how these might be met; the needs, including the developmental needs, of the adoptive child and how these might be met; the parenting capacity of the adoptive parents; and wider family and environmental factors (ASSR 14). Assessments must also consider, in the case of a child who is placed for adoption or matched for adoption by an agency, the circumstances that led to the child being placed or matched, and any previous assessment of adoption support services needs that was undertaken in relation to this child.

Statutory Guidance 2005 requires that these factors reflect those to be considered in assessments carried out under the practice guidance on 'Assessing the support needs of adoptive families', intended as a tool for practitioners undertaking assessments for adoption support services. Local authorities also have the power to assess adoption support service needs at the same time as undertaking another assessments (e.g. for community support services for a person with disabilities) to avoid duplicating assessments.

If needs identified during an assessment relate to services provided by bodies other than local authorities with social service responsibilities and it appears that there may be service implications for health or education services, the local authority is required to consult the relevant Primary Health Trust or Local Education Authority during the assessment (ASR 14).

In nearly all circumstances, it will be appropriate for the person being assessed to be interviewed and this is required by ASR 14. An assessment is not necessary before providing advice and information. It may be possible for an assessment solely concerned with financial support to be conducted by correspondence.

Where the person being assessed is an adoptive child then the adoptive parents may also be interviewed, depending both on the circumstances, and the age and understanding of the child.

5

Discretion to provide support services to individual families

Local authorities must provide adoption support services generally in their area and the range of those services is set out below. However, provision of those services to individual families is at the local authority's discretion. Having assessed an adoptive family and identified what need for services they have, the local authority must make a decision about whether or not to provide services. However, if a local authority's decision not to provide support services is unreasonable, it can be challenged (see chapter 9).

English local authorities are required to ensure that the adoption support services provided to any person are appropriate, having regard to the need for such services identified by an assessment carried out by (or commissioned by) the local authority (LAAS 2003, Regulation 9a (as amended in 2005)).

In other words, if the result of the assessment is that there are needs to be met, the local authority must ensure appropriate services are provided to meet those needs.

Notice of the outcome of assessment

Following the assessment, a person who has been assessed must be given notice by the local authority of the outcome of their assessment, and before making any decision as to whether to provide adoption support services, the local authority must allow that person the opportunity to make representations (ASR 17). The person must be informed, when the notice is given, of the time allowed for making representations.

The notice must contain the following:
1. A statement as to the person's needs for adoption support services.
2. Where the assessment relates to their need for financial support, the basis upon which financial support is determined.
3. Whether the local authority proposes to provide them with adoption support services the services (if any) that are proposed to be provided.
4. If financial support is to be paid, the proposed amount that would be payable; and any conditions attached to the payment (ASR 17).

Notice of a proposal to provide support services

Where the local authority proposes to provide adoption support services and is required to prepare a plan, (see below) the notice must be accompanied by a draft of that plan.

The regulations do not specify a period of time to be allowed for representations, but the DfES suggest in statutory guidance that for assessments carried out on request, a period of 28 days from the time the proposed decision was sent to the applicants is good practice. Where assessments are undertaken before the matching panel the local authority's proposals regarding the provision of adoption support services will be part of the Adoption Placement Report (see chapter 4). This allows 10 working days before the matching panel for the adopters to consider the report and make any representations.

Deciding whether to provide adoption services

After considering any representations received, the local authority must decide whether to provide any services to the person who has been assessed, taking into account the circumstances of the case and the locally available resources.

The local authority cannot make a decision until the person has either commented to or notified the local authority that they are satisfied with the proposed decision and draft plan (if applicable), or the appropriate period of time has expired.

In the case of a decision in an assessment before matching panel, the local authority decision about adoption support should be taken at the same time as the decision about the proposed placement, after consideration of the placement by the adoption panel, and will need to take account of any advice given by the panel about support.

Notice of the decision and the adoption support plan

Having made a decision about what, if any, service to provide, the local authority is then required to give notice of that decision, including the reasons for it (ASR 18).

In the case of a 'matching' assessment, the decision on the provision of adoption support services will be notified alongside the agency's decision that the child be placed with the prospective adopters, and included in the Adoption Placement Plan before placement (see chapter 4). The notice must include the plan and the name of the person nominated to monitor the provision of services within it.

5

If the local authority decides that financial support is to be provided the notice given must include the following:

a) the method of the determination of the amount of financial support.

b) where financial support is to be paid in instalments or periodically;

   the amount of financial support.

   the frequency with which the payment will be made.

   the period for which financial support is to be paid.

   when the first payment of financial support is to be made.

c) where financial support is to be paid as a single payment, when the payment is to be made.

d) where financial support is to be paid subject to any conditions, those conditions, the date (if any) by which the conditions are to be met and the consequences of failing to meet the conditions.

e) the arrangements and procedure for review, variation and termination of financial support.

f) the responsibilities of the local authority in relation to reviews and the adoptive parents in relation to any agreed conditions (ASR 18).

Where service providers other than social services have been involved in the assessment of support needs, the local authority should try, wherever possible, to ensure that decisions made by those service providers follow the same timetable as decisions made under this regulation. These should then be covered in a single notification and plan sent out by the local authority that sets out decisions for the whole service package wherever possible.

The range of adoption support services

The Adoption Support Services Regulations 2005 specify the range of services which a local authority must make available generally in their area to meet the needs of people affected by adoption. These are:

• Financial support (ASSR 2005, 3.1.a) (discussed below).

• Services to enable groups of adopted children, adoptive parents and birth parents or former guardians of an adoptive child to discuss matters relating to adoption (ASSR 2005, 3.1.b).

• Assistance, including mediation services, in relation to contact between an adopted child and a birth parent, birth sibling, former guardian or a related person (ASSR 2005, 3.1 c).

• Therapeutic services for adopted children (ASSR 2005, 3.1.d) (discussed below).

- Assistance to ensure a continued relationship between an adopted child and adoptive parents, (ASSR 2005, 3.1.e), including training for adoptive parents to meet any special needs of the child, and respite care. This can include assistance in cash, for example, giving an adoptive parent money to pay a babysitter so they can have a break. If a child needs respite care by living outside the adoptive home, arrangements by a local authority must involve the child being 'looked after' for the duration of the respite care. This requires that appropriate safeguards are in place. However, being 'looked after' for respite care does not mean the child has been removed from their adopters, or the adoption has failed. It simply means that the local authority must 'look after' the child, i.e. ensure their welfare whilst in respite care.
- Assistance where disruption of an adoptive placement or adoption has occurred, or is in danger of occurring, including making arrangements for providing mediation services and organising and running meetings to discuss disruptions (ASSR 2005, 3.1.f).
- Counselling, advice and information (ASSR 2005, 3.1).

Financial support

ASSR 2005, 8 sets out the circumstances in which financial support may be paid to adoptive parents. These are (author's italics):

a) where it is necessary to ensure that the adoptive parent can look after the child *(to overcome financial obstacles to a child being adopted).*

b) where the child needs special care which requires greater expenditure of resources because of illness, disability, emotional or behavioural difficulties, or the continuing consequences of past abuse or neglect. This financial support is where the child's condition is serious and long-term. For example, the child needs a special diet or items such as shoes or bedding need to be replaced at a higher rate than for a child of similar age unaffected by the particular condition *(and also, for example, to fund treatment or therapy).*

c) where it is necessary for the local authority to make special arrangements to facilitate the placement or the adoption because of the age or ethnic origin of the child *(to ensure there are no financial obstacles to the most appropriate placement of the child).*

d) where it is desirable for the child to be placed with the same adoptive parents as siblings (whether of full or half-blood) or a child with whom they previously shared a home *(for example, an extension to provide room for a sibling group)*.

e) where the support is to meet recurring costs for travel for the purpose of visits between the child and a related person *(contact arrangements)*.

f) where the local authority considers it appropriate to make a contribution to meet the following kinds of expenditure:

(i) legal costs, including fees payable to a court in relation to an adoption *(including the costs of separate legal representation for adopters)*.

(ii) for the purpose of introducing an adoptive child to their adoptive parents *(for example travel and hotel costs)*.

(iii) expenditure needed for accommodating and maintaining the child, including furniture and domestic equipment, adaptations of the home, means of transport, and clothing, toys and other items necessary for looking after the child *(settling-in grant)*.

Remuneration for former foster carers

Financial support cannot normally include the payment of remuneration (i.e. fees or salaries) to adoptive parents. (ASSR 2005, 9). However, where the adoptive parents previously fostered the child they are adopting, and they received remuneration as the child's foster parents, the local authority may continue to pay that remuneration for two years from the date of the adoption order. The two year period is to give the family time to adjust to their new financial circumstances. The payment of remuneration can continue for longer than two years if the local authority considers the case to be exceptional.

Payment of financial support

ASSR 2005, 10 provides that financial support may be paid periodically, as a regular allowance, if it is paid to meet a need which is likely to lead to recurring expenditure. In other cases it may be paid as a single payment or, if the local authority and adoptive parents agree, in instalments.

Cessation (stopping) of financial support

Financial support ceases to be payable to adoptive parents if:

a) the child ceases to have a home with them.

b) the child ceases full-time education or training and commences employment.

c) the child qualifies for Income Support or Jobseeker's Allowance in their own right.

d) the child reaches the age of 18 unless they continue in full-time education or training, when it may continue until the end of the course or training (ASSR 2005, 11).

Financial support paid as an allowance – conditions and annual statements

Where financial support is to be paid as a regular ongoing allowance the adoptive parents must agree:

a) that they will inform the local authority immediately if they change address, the child dies, if any of the changes mentioned in ASSR 2005, 11 (cessation of financial support) occur; or if there is a change in the adopters' financial circumstances or the financial needs or resources of the child which may affect the amount of financial support payable.

b) Where the information is given orally, the adopters will confirm it in writing within seven days.

c) To complete and supply the local authority with an annual statement as to their and their child's financial circumstances, their address and whether the child still has a home with them (ASSR 2005, 12).

The local authority may set any other conditions they consider appropriate, including the timescale within which and purposes for which any payment of financial support should be utilised. An example might be that if money is provided to fund the building of an extension or the purchase of a bigger house for a large sibling group, the prospective adopters would enter into a legal agreement so that the local authority would be refunded from the sale of the house if the placement broke down within a short period (ASSR 2005, 12).

If this kind of agreement is suggested, prospective adopters should be given funding by the local authority for separate legal advice before entering into the agreement. Where any condition imposed is not complied with, the local authority may suspend or terminate payment of financial support and seek to recover all or part of the financial support they have paid.

Financial support – implications for adopters

There is no automatic entitlement to financial support

Whilst a child or adoptive family might meet one or more of the criteria for financial support, it may not be paid if the local authority considers that the adoptive family does not qualify for financial support, or it is available from other sources such as benefits or tax credits.

Adopters must be open about their financial circumstances

Adopters are legally obliged to provide full details of their income and expenditure to the local authority, both when financial support is being considered and at the obligatory annual reviews.

Local authority financial support must complement not duplicate that available from other sources

Local authorities must ensure adoptive families are aware of, and take advantage of, all benefits and tax credits available to them. However, local authorities can fill any gaps in other provision, for example paid adoption leave not being available to the self-employed.

The means test

When considering providing financial support, the local authority will usually assess the adoptive family's financial circumstances. ASSR 2005, 15 requires that the local authority considers:

a) the adoptive parents' financial resources (including significant income from any investments, but not the value of their home) including any tax credit or benefit which would be available to them if a child is placed.

b) the amount required by the adoptive parents in respect of reasonable outgoings and commitments e.g. housing and transport costs and daily living expenses (but excluding outgoings in respect of the child).

c) the financial needs (e.g. because of special diet or need for replacement bedding) and the child's financial resources (e.g. a trust fund).

Currently each local authority applies its own means test which leads to the possibility of a 'postcode lottery', with some local authorities applying a more generous means test than others. A suggested means test was published on the DfES website in August 2005, which local authorities may use. This marks a possible move towards a standard means test required to be used by all local authorities in the future.

The local authority must disregard an adoptive family's financial resources where they are considering providing money for the initial costs of accommodating the child – a settling-in grant for furniture and equipment. (ASSR 2005, 15) However local authorities may apply the means test to assess any contribution by the adoptive family to an adaptation or extension to the home, if the purchase of the adaptation or extension is to be funded by financial support given to the adopters, rather than purchased or supplied directly by the local authority.

In deciding the amount of financial support the local authority must also take into account any advice given by their adoption panel. The decision whether or not to provide financial support to adopters rests with the local authority, and the amount paid is also discretionary. Each local authority may pay at a different rate, can change schemes and must alter them in response to new legislation. However, they must inform adopters of proposed changes and give them an opportunity to comment.

It may (depending on individual circumstances) be possible to enforce the agreement to provide financial support as a legal contract, so that if local authorities agree to make payments and then without good reason do not, they can be challenged (see chapter 9). However it would be wise to bear in mind that the level and the duration of payments can vary over time. Therefore adopters need to be very careful about the exact terms of an agreement before relying on it in making long term financial plans and may need to take legal advice about the terms of a plan for financial support.

5

At all times local authorities must act reasonably in making their decisions and can be challenged about decisions which seem unfair or unreasonable. However, any claim that the local authority has been unreasonable may be invalidated if adopters have failed to supply financial information or concealed some of their resources.

Financial support to adopters from other sources

Adoption paid leave for employees

Information is available from the DTI booklet 'Adoptive Parents; rights to leave and pay when a child is placed for adoption in the UK'. Proposals (for consultation) were published in January 2006 to extend statutory adoption pay from 26 to 39 weeks from April 2007. More information is available from the DTI website.

Child Tax Credits and Working Tax Credit

Income based support for families with children can be claimed from the Inland Revenue from the date of placement for adoption.

Disregard for Income Tax and Tax Credits and Benefits

Financial support for adopters is disregarded when determining eligibility to tax credits, and is disregarded (except the child and disabled child premium) for calculating income for the purposes of income related benefits (Jobseeker's Allowance, Housing Benefit, Income Support, and Council Tax benefit).
Financial support to adopters is also exempt from income tax.

Child Benefit

Child Benefit, administered by the Inland Revenue, is available from the date of placement for adoption. The Benefits Agency provides a general guide for parents to benefits and tax credits, in the form of leaflet 'BC1 – Babies and Children'.

Responsibility for providing support services to adopters

Local authorities have a legal responsibility to provide adoption support services generally in their area. Section 3(4) of ACA 2002 enables a local authority to arrange for adoption support services to be provided by other organisations on its behalf, including registered adoption societies, registered adoption support agencies, other local authorities, Primary Care Trusts (Local Health Boards in Wales) and Local Education Authorities (LEAs).

Therefore local authorities can contract these organisations to provide an adoption support service. However, a local authority cannot require another organisation or authority to provide that service.

Whilst health and education services are provided free of charge to families in their areas, there will be times when the services which individual adoptive families are assessed as needing, e.g. specialist therapy or education provision, are not available from the local Primary Care Trust or LEAs.

The regulations are clear that the legal responsibility to secure the provision of these services for individual adoptive families, if the local authority assessed them as needed, rests with the local authority. The authority must find a way of achieving the provision by contracting with other organisations – private as well as public.

The financial burden on local authorities is made heavier if Primary Care Trusts and LEAs do not provide the specialist services which are expected of them. This issue is politically controversial and sensitive. It is also the reason why some adoptive families experience delay and frustration in accessing services, particularly therapeutic help. However, it is clear from the support regulations that ultimately responsibility for adoption support provision lies with local authorities.

Providing services to non-agency adoptive families

Apart from stepparent adopters, the local authority where non-agency adoptive families live is required to extend all of its adoption support services to them (although it is a condition of approval of most intercountry adopters that they do not need financial support at the approval or placement stages).

The local authority is only required to extend counselling, advice and information services to stepparent adopters. However a local authority has discretion to extend their services as it considers appropriate, for example to prevent disruption in a stepparent adoptive family, or to give financial support to an intercountry adoptive family.

Providing support to agency adoptive families – which local authority?

The three year rule (ASSR 2005, 7)

The local authority which placed the child with the adopters is responsible for the assessment on request of support needs, and provision of support services, wherever the adoptive family live, for the first three years after adoption orders are granted.

Three years after the adoption order is made, the local authority where the adoptive family lives is responsible for assessing and providing support services.

An exception to the three year rule

Where financial support is paid as a regular allowance, beginning before the adoption order is granted, the assessment and provision of this support remains the responsibility of the local authority who originally agreed it (the placing local authority), for as long after the adoption order as the family qualifies for these payments.

The Adoption Support Services Adviser (ASSR 2005, 6)

All local authorities are required to appoint an Adoption Support Services Adviser (ASSA), whose role is to give advice and information to people affected by adoption – a single point of contact to provide information, signpost appropriate services and to advise on how those services may be accessed.

"The appointment of an ASSA provides clarity for adoptive parents about who in the authority to approach for advice, and identifies a first port of call for questions about adoption support services, the process for accessing support and queries in relation to existing support arrangements." (Adoption Guidance 2005 (statutory))

Contact details for the ASSA should be publicised to make it easier for adoptive families seeking help and advice. ASSAs should encourage adopters to access the support services that are available, including mainstream and specialist adoption-focused services. They should also signpost adopters to information about other forms of

5

support that might be available to them, for example, tax credits and benefits. Where appropriate, ASSAs should act as advocates, for example, liaising with education or health services on behalf of a recipient of adoption support services.

While queries on existing adoption support plans should normally be referred to the named lead person for that plan (as required by ASSR 2005, 16) the ASSA may have a role to play in resolving queries, in particular where these relate to provision of services by other agencies. Requests for assessments of adoption support needs that come to the ASSA should be passed on promptly to an appropriate social worker to carry out the assessment. The ASSA should then provide advice about issues such as the services and resources available locally, the way in which assessments should be undertaken, and processes for planning, decisions and reviews.

Skills and knowledge required of the ASSA

The local authority must only appoint a person as an ASSA who has sufficient knowledge and experience to perform their role effectively. The ASSA will need to have good knowledge and experience of the adoption process, and the impact of adoption on all parties involved. ASSR 2005, 6 makes this a condition of appointment.

The ASSA will also need to develop a good knowledge of relevant services in the area, both within social services and other relevant local agencies.

Further implications for adopters

The experience of adoptive families since the implementation of the first Adoption Support Regulations in October 2003 has been mixed. Some receive very good support services, for some the provision of support plans and services has been patchy or inadequate, for others no support plans were made before placement. In the worst cases, some adoptive families struggle even to get an assessment of their support needs, or local authorities fail to provide support services which are urgently needed. Sadly for some families the lack of provision of support, particularly therapy for children, or respite for the adopters, can lead to placements breaking down.

Sometimes the failure to provide services is because social workers are unaware of the legal obligations imposed upon them by regulations, other times because local authorities choose to keep their adopters in the dark concerning their entitlement to support plans and assessment, and from time to time because they know their legal obligations but try to avoid them.

The financial and staffing burdens for local authorities are considerable, but local authorities are given money by central government for adoption support, and are obliged in law to provide adoption support services and to appoint ASSAs to ensure that adopters have a single point of contact and a source of help – as a 'broker' with other agencies, and a 'trouble shooter'.

Well-supported adoptive families are likely to be more successful than those who are let down and vulnerable because support is not provided. One likely result of support not being provided can be disrupted adoptions, and these cause even greater financial costs to local authorities, aside from the grief and distress caused to families and children.

This chapter makes prospective adopters aware of their rights and the legal obligations of local authorities towards them, and so able to assert their needs more effectively. Chapter 9 sets out how local authorities can be challenged about adoption support issues.

5

Contact and adoptive placements

It is very clear from social work practice and research that contact arrangements which can be agreed and are mutually acceptable between adoptive and birth families (and where appropriate and possible the children as well), are far more likely to succeed than those imposed by a court making contact orders.

This chapter sets out the law in relation to contact and adoption and the implications for adopters. The ACA 2002 recognises the significance for most children's emotional well-being of relationships with birth parents and others (Section 1 (4)(f) of the welfare checklist). However it also recognises the need for legal certainty about contact arrangements for children authorised to be placed for adoption and in adoptive placements, and that for some children contact is not in their best interests. The Act provides a new regime (Section 26 contact) which governs contact after a child has been authorised to be placed for adoption and before the adoption order.

Types of contact

Contact can take a number of forms. Direct contact is face to face meetings or other first hand contact such as phone calls, text messaging and emails, between a child and their birth parents, siblings and other birth family members, or people significant to the child, including previous foster carers. Sometimes this contact is supervised by professionals or the adoptive parents.

Indirect contact is communications such as cards, letters and information exchanges between adoptive and birth families, and other people significant to the child. This is usually via a social services 'letterbox' system whereby the adoptive family's identity and location (and the adopted child's new name) can remain confidential. It is rare for people to be approved as agency adopters unless they are at least willing to participate in and allow indirect contact after adoption.

Contact between adoptive and birth families may also be arranged between themselves without help or intervention from social services or the need for court orders.

Contact and non-agency adoptions

Before the adoption order

Children being adopted by their stepparents, relatives, or private foster carers may or may not be subject of contact orders (Children Act 1989, Section 8). For example, after birth parents separate or divorce, the child might live with one parent and an order made in favour of the other parent to ensure contact takes place. The Section 8 order (if any), and to whom it has been granted, will determine who has contact with the child, and may specify how, when and where contact is to take place (known as a 'defined' contact order).

It would be unusual for a court to grant an adoption order to non-agency adopters such as stepparents if the birth parent not living with the child has been granted a Section 8 contact order. The court's reluctance to make an adoption order in these circumstances is because of the recognition that after the separation of their parents, contact with both birth parents is usually crucial to a child's emotional welfare. The adoption order would discharge the contact order and so might end one parent's entitlement to that contact.

Where parents are having contact without an order having being granted (for example by mutual agreement between divorced parents, or where their child is living with private foster carers) courts are also reluctant to grant adoption orders if is likely that the adopters would refuse contact to the birth parents.

Looked after children being adopted by their local authority foster carers without the support of the local authority may be the subject of contact orders under Section 34 (3) of the Children Act 1989 (which covers contact to children in care). Granting an adoption order would discharge the Section 34 order and the court considering if the adoption order was in the child's best interests would have to take this into account. However, a contact order under Section 8 of CA 1989 could be granted with the adoption order.

Contact and looked after children before adoptive placement

Chapter 3 described the legal circumstances of children looked after by a local authority. Until a child is legally authorised to be placed for adoption the authority is legally obliged to provide and promote reasonable contact between these children and their birth parents and must consider the child's needs to have contact with siblings, other birth family members, or significant others.

Contact for a child placed for adoption under six weeks of age with parental agreement

The duty for a local authority to provide and promote contact to a looked after child does not apply if a child is placed for adoption by an agency under six weeks of age, with the agreement of the parents. Contact is at the discretion of the local authority, or parents or guardians, and (close) relatives can apply for contact orders under Section 26 of ACA 2002.

Contact to children authorised to be placed for adoption

Looked after children become authorised to be placed for adoption by section 19 parental consent or by a court granting a placement order. After authorisation, there is no duty for the local authority looking after the child to promote or provide contact. Contact is at the discretion of the local authority or parents and (close) relatives can apply for contact orders under Section 26 of ACA 2002.

Section 26 contact order

This order requires the person with whom the child lives or is to live, to allow the child to visit or stay with the person named in the order. Alternatively, the order could allow the person named in the order and the child to have other forms of contact with each other. This order could therefore apply to both direct and indirect contact.

The person with whom the child lives or is to live may be the child's foster carers before placement for adoption, but also includes prospective adopters who have been approached about or matched with a child, or with whom the child has been placed.

6

An adoption agency must make its decisions about contact arrangements for authorised children after taking into account the welfare checklist (especially Section 1[4] [f], see chapter 3), the wishes and feelings of the birth family members, and any advice given by the adoption panel when it makes the 'should be placed for adoption' and 'matching with adoptive family' recommendations (AAR 2005, 46).

Section 26 contact orders at the making of a placement order

Section 26 contact orders can be applied for when an application is made for a placement order by any of the following without leave of court; the child or local authority, any parent, guardian or (close) relative, and any person who has a Children Act 1989 contact order (Section 8 or Section 34) or a residence order before the placement order is made. Close relatives are grandparents, siblings, aunts or uncles (full or half blood, or by marriage), or civil partnership.

Anyone else may apply for Section 26 contact orders with the court's permission, e.g. prospective adopters with whom the child will live if the placement order is made, or with whom the child is already living (i.e. foster carers). The court hearing the application for a placement order must also consider what, if any, contact orders might be in the interests of the child. The court can make Section 26 contact orders on its own initiative, without anyone applying for an order.

If no Section 26 contact order is made with the placement order, the local authority is not obliged to provide contact, although it may do so if it is considered to be in the interests of the child.

Implications when placements are proposed

When placement orders are applied for there are usually no prospective adopters identified for the child (unless the child is being adopted by their foster carers or the plan is for the child to join a family who have adopted their older siblings). Thus a court considering making a Section 26 order with the placement order will not be able to take into account the views of the prospective adopters for the child. However, any Section 26 order should be for contact arrangements which are likely to be compatible with the child's needs in the present and the future, including the need for an adoptive family. The contact arrangements and/or orders should not be an obstacle to finding adopters.

Prospective adopters who see a child 'advertised' as needing an adoptive family should ask whether any Section 26 contact orders have been made with the placement order (or are being applied for in the placement order proceedings) and for what level and kind of contact. This is crucial because prospective adopters must comply with Section 26 contact orders during placement, unless they are varied or revoked.

Varying or revoking Section 26 contact orders

At any time after a Section 26 contact order is made, it can be varied (for example reducing or increasing the level of contact) or revoked (ended), by the child or local authority, any parent, guardian or (close) relative, and any person who had a Section 8 or Section 34 contact order or a residence order before the placement order was made, applying to the court. The court's permission is not needed for these people to apply to change or revoke Section 26 contact orders.

If the adoption agency proposes to make any change to the contact arrangements it must seek the views of the child (if the agency consider they are of sufficient age and understanding), their parents or guardians, any person who had a Section 8 or Section 34 contact order, and any other person the agency considers relevant, as well as the prospective adopters. It must take all their views into account when deciding what arrangements it should make for contact with the child while they are placed for adoption.

Prospective adopters with whom the child is living or is to live may also apply for Section 26 contact orders - including an order for no contact, if they have the court's permission to make the application.

Contact and planning adoptive placements - consulting the prospective adopters

The adoption agency must set out the contact arrangements in the Adoption Placement Report and the Adoption Placement Plan (see chapter 4) and keep them under review.

AAR 2005, 46 (5) requires that when an adoption agency decides to place a child with particular adopters, the agency must review the contact arrangements, including Section 26 contact orders before placement, in the light of the views of the prospective adopters and any advice given by the adoption panel at the matching stage.

Implications for adopters before placement

Chapter 4 sets out how prospective adopters learn about the proposed contact arrangements when they are first approached about a child (the Child's Permanence Report), and their views about these proposed arrangements must be taken into account when the placement is being planned; specifically in the Adoption Placement Report before matching panel.

The matching adoption panel will advise the agency about the proposed contact arrangements that take into account the prospective adopters views, contained in the Adoption Placement Report. The regulatory requirements are clear that if Section 26 contact orders are granted, or contact arrangements made by agreement, prior to adoptive placement, these arrangements or orders can be changed or varied. These changes or variation would be to ensure they fit with the child's needs, which may have changed since the placement order was made or might change in the future, and the prospective adopter's views at placement stage.

The possible difficulties to this procedure are firstly that the need to go back to court to vary or revoke Section 26 contact orders before placement may delay the placement. This might be avoided if local authorities are careful to ensure that Section 26 contact orders made with placement orders are designed to allow for future developments – such as having to adapt the arrangements to take into account changes in the child's needs or wishes, and the views of the prospective adopters when they are identified.

The second difficulty is that it may not be straightforward to vary or revoke Section 26 contact orders or contact agreements made prior to an adoptive family being found, even if they are not compatible with the views of the prospective adopters. This may be because the local authority does not support the proposed changes despite the views of the prospective adopters. It may also be because parents and others successfully resist any applications to revoke or vary orders made in their favour at the placement order stage - or attempts to renegotiate agreements.

If this situation arises, the prospective adopters can ask the court for permission to make their own application for a Section 26 contact order, but if they are not supported by the child's local authority, they would probably have to fund their own legal representation for making the application. The alternative for prospective adopters is to decline to accept the placement until and unless the contact arrangements are acceptable to them.

Contact during adoptive placements

Prospective adopters must comply with Section 26 contact orders in force at the time of placement, during the placement and up to the making of the adoption order, unless they are varied or revoked. At any time after a Section 26 contact order is made, it can be varied or revoked, by the child or local authority, any parent, guardian or (close) relative, and any person who had a Section 8 or Section 34 contact order or a residence order before the placement order was made, applying to the court. The court's permission is not needed for these people to apply to change or revoke Section 26 contact orders.

Anyone else may apply for a Section 26 order, including an order for no contact, with the permission of the court, including the child's prospective adopters. Since they have parental responsibility for the child during the placement this permission may be simple to obtain.

Implications during adoptive placement

Above are the legal avenues open to local authorities and children, parents, relatives and some others, and (with permission of the court) prospective adopters, to change Section 26 contact orders during an adoptive placement. If local authorities and prospective adopters agree about the changes needed, achieving them should be relatively straightforward despite involving a court application, and it would be reasonable for prospective adopters of a looked after child to expect the child's local authority to make and progress any application. If the local authority and the prospective adopters disagree, changes will be more difficult, due to the need for prospective adopters to seek permission of the court to make the application, and the probable lack of financial and other support from the authority.

Also set out above are the ways in which parents and others, without needing the permission of the court, can make and

6

continue to make applications for Section 26 contact orders during adoptive placement. The latter may be a cause for concern to prospective adopters, as it may never be possible to know if their placement will be untroubled or very troubled by such applications. It is hard to offer reassurance or advice to adopters – this is very new law, and it is not possible to know if courts will be swift to stop repeated unsettling applications by parents or others who cannot reconcile themselves to their child's adoption.

However, prospective adopters are entitled to help from the children's local authorities (and any CAFCASS officers appointed in the contact proceedings), if such applications are likely to be adverse to the welfare of the child.

This chapter and chapter 4 describe how contact arrangements and orders can be planned and changed before placement. This is a crucial time for ensuring that contact arrangements are compatible with the child's life in a new family, and for contingency plans to protect placements to be built in before placement. Chapter 7 describes how contact arrangements, including Section 26 contact orders, must be reviewed during adoptive placement by an Independent Reviewing Officer. This officer has a duty to try to resolve problems to protect and enhance the child's welfare and progress their care plan, and if necessary, help a child initiate legal action. This might include a child applying for a contact order, or a variation or revocation of a Section 26 contact order.

Emergency suspension of contact

The local authority looking after the child may suspend contact for a maximum of seven days contrary to a Section 26 order, if this is urgently required in the interests of the child.

Departing from the terms of a Section 26 contact order

Section 26 contact orders can be departed from if the local authority and the persons in whose favour the contact order was made agree.

Contact orders after adoption or with an adoption order

Section 8 of the CA 1989 and Section 46[6] of the ACA 2002 provide for contact orders for children who have been adopted or when an adoption order is granted. These orders have been available since 1991, but are very rarely granted.

During adoptive placements

This chapter covers the time from children first joining their agency adoptive families up to the granting of adoption orders, setting out the legal obligations of adoption agencies to visit and review placements under the Adoption Agencies Regulations 2005 (AAR 2005), and clarifying who makes which decisions about children before the adoption order.

The legal circumstances of children placed with agency adopters

The vast majority of children placed with agency prospective adopters will be the subject of placement orders. The remainder will be children relinquished for adoption after formal parental consent to placement has been given. The legal consequences are set out in detail in chapter 3. They include parental responsibility being shared between birth parents, prospective adopters and children's local authorities, and contact arrangements governed by Section 26 contact orders (see chapter 6). There are also some limited opportunities for parents and guardians to have children they relinquished for adoption returned to them, or for parents or guardians to oppose the making of adoption orders.

(For a year or two after 30 December 2005, due to an overlap in the laws, some children in placement will have freeing for adoption orders, where neither the birth parents or the prospective adopters have parental responsibility for the child. Birth parents and relatives of 'freed' children are not entitled to apply for Section 26 contact orders, nor can parents apply for leave to oppose adoption orders being made.)

Parental responsibility during placement

Agency prospective adopters will have parental responsibility for the children from the date of placement (unless a child is placed with them under six weeks of age). Parental responsibility will be shared with the child's agency and the birth parents or guardians, although the latter will have their entitlement to exercise parental responsibility severely limited.

Chapter 4 described how agreements are reached before placement about the extent to which prospective adopters will have parental responsibility for the child delegated to them, and this must be set out in the Adoption Placement Plan provided to the adopters before placement. The delegation could include making decisions about routine medical treatment, education, overnight stays, taking the child abroad for less than one month, change of forename etc. Therefore it should be clear to prospective adopters which decisions they can take, and which they should refer to the child's agency. The extent of delegation of parental responsibility must be reviewed at regular intervals (see below) and can be altered if necessary, or if there are concerns about the decisions proposed or made.

There are two decisions which neither the child's agency nor the prospective adopters may take even though they now have parental responsibility – causing a child to be known by a new surname and taking the child out of the UK for more than one month. Both need the permission of a court, or the written permission of each parent or guardian with parental responsibility. Chapter 5 discusses changing a child's name before or during adoptive placement.

The decision to apply for the adoption order

Agency adopters cannot apply for the adoption order until the child has lived with them for at least 10 weeks. The decision to apply is for the prospective adopters to take. However it is best taken in consultation with their social worker and the child's social worker when all, including the child (with sufficient understanding), agree that the time is right. This decision by the prospective adopters may be at or following a review of the placement, but it is not the reviewing officer's or the local authority's decision.

As chapters 8 and 9 show, sadly sometimes the decision to apply for the adoption order will not come out of consensus, but be driven by other considerations, including avoiding the child being removed from the adoptive placement or disputes about contact or support.

Visits to adoptive families during placements

Frequency of visits

The child and the prospective adopters must be visited by the agency
social workers within a week of the placement, and at least once a
week until the first review at four weeks. The frequency of visits is
then decided by the agency at the first and subsequent reviews.

Which social worker visits?

Visits should be shared wherever possible between the child's social
worker and the prospective adopters' social worker and it should be
clear from the outset which social worker will make each visit.
Where the child is placed outside the area of the child's agency,
and/or the child's social worker cannot visit the placement, the child's
agency should make arrangements with another agency to ensure a
social worker visits the placement.

Seeing the child alone

The visiting social worker should see the child without the
prospective adopters being present, unless the child is of sufficient
age and understanding and refuses to see the social worker alone.

Reports of visits

The agency must ensure that written reports are made of all visits
and both the child's and prospective adopters' social workers should
write reports of their visits and share these with the other social
worker. (AAR 2005, 36.4)

Advice and assistance for prospective adopters

The agency must provide advice and assistance to the prospective
adopters it thinks necessary and as proposed before the placement
in the Adoption Placement Plan. They also have a legal right to a
reassessment of their support needs by the child's local authority at
any time during the placement (see chapter 5).

Advice and assistance for children in placements

Children in agency adoptive placements are still looked after and
their local authority continues to have the full range of duties towards
them, including safeguarding their welfare and promoting their
educational achievement. Before making any decision local authorities

7

must, as far as is practicable, ascertain the wishes and feelings of the child, and take these into account (bearing in mind their age and understanding). They must also consider the child's religious persuasion, racial origin, and cultural and linguistic backgrounds.

Implications for adopters

The frequency of visits set by regulations to prospective adopters with children in placement are minimum requirements for adoption agencies. Many prospective adopters will receive, and welcome, more frequent visits. The Adoption Placement Plan (chapter 4) will contain the out of hours contact details for their and the child's social workers, if urgent visits or advice is required.

The term 'visits' perhaps glosses over their purpose; they are not social occasions, they are legally required opportunities for the social workers to check on the welfare of children living with their new families, and to judge how the prospective adopters are adjusting and coping in their new roles as parents. Research and experience suggest that a placement is at its most vulnerable and most likely to disrupt in the first few weeks, hence the requirement to visit weekly for the first four weeks.

Many issues may arise in adoptive placements that the prospective adopters and sometimes the children need help, advice and support with. Examples may include the child's behaviour or emotional state, health concerns, adoption support which has been promised but not been provided, contact arrangements which are unsuccessful, and sometimes relationships between the prospective adopters running into difficulties. Sadly, relationships between social workers and prospective adopters sometimes need help, advice and support too (see reviews in this chapter, and chapter 9). Sometimes even the minimum required visits do not occur, or are hasty and ill planned, especially those by overburdened local authority social workers. These give the prospective adopters little opportunity to air any concerns or needs they have. In addition in some cases the child's social worker is insensitive or unhelpful. In these circumstances prospective adopters are usually able to rely on their own social worker, from the agencies which approved them, to try to get the help and assistance needed by negotiation or 'chivvying' the child's agency. The system of reviewing placements

7

and the role of the Independent Reviewing Officer should also provide avenues for remedying these problems.

Statutory reviews of adoptive placements

AAR 2005, 36 requires that a reviewing officer independent of the child or prospective adopters' agency (the IRO) must ensure that reviews of children in adoptive placement are held at the required intervals and, as far as is practicable, attend and chair the reviews.

The agency should provide written information about how it intends to review placements. This should be given to prospective adopters in the Adoption Placement Plan, to the child where the agency considers they are of sufficient age and understanding, and to anyone else the agency considers relevant, such as the child's parents or guardians.

Reviews may be held in the prospective adopters' home and if the location or identity of the adoptive family is not to be known to the parents or guardians they will not be invited to attend these reviews. However they may be asked to give their views about issues which are to be discussed at reviews such as any contact arrangements. Where parents, guardians or other persons are considered to be necessary participants in a review the meetings may need to be arranged for a venue outside the adoptive home. There will of course be some reviews where the birth and adoptive families know each other and are comfortable with both participating in the reviews.

7

Frequency of reviews

The first review should be held not more than four weeks after the date the child is placed for adoption. Subsequent reviews should be held not more than three months after the first review, and then not more than six months after the date of the previous review, until an adoption order is granted. The agency may conduct additional reviews where it considers it appropriate, including at the request of the prospective adopters or child.

Ascertaining views

When carrying out a review the agency is required by AAR 2005, 36.5 to ascertain the views, so far as is reasonably practicable, of:
1. the child, bearing in mind their age and understanding.
2. the prospective adopters.

3. any other person the agency considers relevant. This might include the child's parents or guardians, if appropriate.

Other persons who may be relevant might be, for example, other children living in the prospective adopter's home, or the child's health visitor, therapist or teacher.

Reports for reviews

Many of the professional people consulted will write reports for the review, and children may be asked to complete some written work too. Prospective adopters may consider writing their own reports, so that their concerns and issues become part of the records of reviews – otherwise they will be reliant on the minutes of reviews (usually written by the IRO) accurately recording the issues they raised.

Content of the reviews

AAR 2005, 36.6 stipulates that the matters to be considered by the agency for the review are:

1. whether the agency remains satisfied that the child should be placed for adoption (i.e. is adoption still the right plan?).
2. the child's needs, welfare and development, and whether any changes need to be made to meet these.
3. the existing arrangements for contact, and whether they should continue or be altered.
4. the arrangements in relation to the exercise of parental responsibility for the child by the adopters and birth parents, and whether they should continue or be altered.
5. the arrangements for the provision of adoption support services to the adoptive family and whether there should be any re-assessment of the need for those services.
6. in consultation with the appropriate agencies, the arrangements to assess and meet the child's health care and educational needs.

Implications for adopters

The agenda for reviews is set out above, but is not an exclusive list and should not be followed so rigidly that other issues relevant to the welfare of the placement are not raised. Prospective adopters (and children) might consider writing down the matters they want discussed at reviews (as well as or instead of their own reports) to ensure that they are included in the review agenda.

Review recommendations and agency decisions

Reviews will make recommendations as to what should happen next, e.g. changing contact or support arrangements, delegation of more parental responsibility to the prospective adopters, or the prospective adopters progressing the adoption order application.

Where any decision is taken by the agency as a result of a review, the agency is required by AAR 2005, 36.8 to notify, so far as is reasonably practicable, the child, where the agency considers they are of sufficient age and understanding, the prospective adopters and any other person the agency considers relevant. This might include the child's parents or guardians if appropriate.

Recording reviews

AAR 2005, 36.9 requires the agency to record in writing and place on the child's case record the detail of a review including:
1. the views expressed by the child.
2. the minutes of any meeting arranged by the agency to consider any aspect of the review.
3. details of any decision made during or as a result of the review.

7

Implications for adopters

Whist review meetings may appear informal chatty occasions, they are required by law to ensure that there are regular formal examinations of the welfare of children in adoptive placements. They also ensure that all those involved – not just the social workers but also the child and prospective adopters – are consulted and given a voice, and are clear about what has been recorded and recommended as a result of the review.

Reviews are valuable opportunities for prospective adopters to raise issues and discuss possible resolutions to problems for the well-being of the placement, and to plan the future. Sadly however, the experience is that some reviews are late, never happen or are too hastily planned or insensitively conducted, or prospective adopters are left in the dark about what was recommended or who is responsible for doing what afterwards. The proper conduct and fairness of reviews should be ensured by the Independent Reviewing Officer who chairs them. Their appointment became a legal requirement in September 2004.

The role of Independent Reviewing Officers (IRO)

AAR 2005, 37.2 and 37.3 stipulate that the Independent Reviewing Officer (IRO) must be a registered social worker and in the opinion of the agency have sufficient relevant social work experience to undertake the role and functions of an IRO. Adoption experience is not however stipulated in the regulations. Some local authorities have appointed IROs with previous adoption experience to specialise in reviewing adoptive placements.

The IROs role includes to participate (and usually chair) the review of a child's case. They have a duty to monitor the implementation of a child's care plan from the perspective of the child's welfare being paramount, "to ensure that plans for looked after children are timely, effective and sensitive to needs", and "correct defects in implementation" (Statutory guidance for IROs). This will include scrutinising how children's local authorities are functioning in terms of carrying out the adoption care plans, including the proposals and commitments set out in the Adoption Placement Plan, contact, adoption support and eventually achieving adoption orders.

AAR 2005, 37.6 requires the IRO to ensure, as far as is reasonably practicable, that reviews are conducted in accordance with AAR 2005, 36 and in particular to ensure that:
1. the children's views are understood and taken into account.
2. anyone responsible for implementing any decision taken as a result of a review is identified.
3. any failure to review a case in accordance with AAR 2005, 36 or to take proper steps to make the arrangements agreed at reviews is brought to the attention of senior managers within the agency.

The child's local authority must inform IROs of any significant failure to make arrangements agreed at reviews, and any significant change in children's circumstances after reviews (AAR 2005, 37.8).

Problem solving by Independent Reviewing Officers

IROs have a legal duty to attempt to resolve problems in the implementation of the care plans for children in adoptive placements, by negotiation with the agencies involved. This negotiation begins at the child's social worker level and must move upwards through the agency hierarchy to the highest level until the problem is resolved.

IROs should inform children of their rights to complaints and advocacy services (see chapter 9). They should also assist the child to obtain legal advice and take legal action and/or establish whether an appropriate adult, (who might be a prospective adopter) is able and willing to bring proceedings on the child's behalf (AAR 2005, 37.7).

If a child wishes to take proceedings on their own account, for example to apply to the court to revoke a placement order or section 26 contact order, the IRO must help the child obtain legal advice, or establish whether an appropriate adult is able and willing to obtain that legal advice or bring the proceedings on the child's behalf. This might include a child taking legal action against their local authority for failure to meet its statutory obligations under the Adoption Agencies Regulations (AAR 2005) or Adoption Support Services Regulations (ASSR 2005) as set out in previous chapters.

Power for IROs to refer a case to CAFCASS Legal Services

If all other methods of resolving a problem are unsuccessful, and where a child's Human Rights are considered to have been breached, IROs should consider referral to CAFCASS Legal "so that legal proceedings can be brought to achieve the outcome sought by, or on behalf of the child" (Statutory Guidance for IROs). Examples might be where the placement is being affected because the local authority is not meeting its obligations for reassessment of support needs, is not providing agreed support e.g. therapy or respite, or contact arrangements are undermining a child's security. Any of these might be considered breaches of the child's Human Right to family life.

CAFCASS Legal will allocate an officer to assess, decide the course of action, and report back to IRO in 14 days. If CAFCASS Legal decides that legal action should be taken on behalf of the child it must issue proceedings within six weeks.

7

Implications for adopters

The independence of IROs and their role and duty to ensure reviews are conducted properly and 'progress chase' adoption care plans for looked after children, should provide 'champions' for these children and their prospective adopters who are faced with difficulties during adoptive placement. In particular prospective adopters and children should be able to rely on IROs to 'trouble shoot' when the child's local authorities are not doing their job well enough. IROs can, for example, be asked by prospective adopters or children to convene extra reviews to bring together all the people involved to try to find a resolution to a problem.

However, snags to the IRO system have often disappointed the high expectations following its introduction in 2004. One obstacle to the IRO system being effective is that many IROs are not really independent of the local authorities they monitor. Although they must not work within the management structure directly responsible for the child's case, most are employed by the same local authority, and may be in the same offices as the child's social worker. In these circumstances challenging the child's social worker or their managers is tricky both professionally and personally.

Although IROs are required to be registered social workers there is no legal requirement to have any adoption social work experience or knowledge, which sometimes leads to insensitivity or mistaken attitudes towards prospective adopters – such as failing to recognise the emotional investment prospective adopters have in their children, compared with that of temporary foster carers. Some IROs are not knowledgeable about adoption law and can make the wrong recommendations as a result, or fail to understand the legal obligations of local authorities towards prospective adopters and children in adoptive placements. For example they may believe they have the right to decide when an adoption order application should be made, or may not identify a lack of provision of adoption support agreed to be provided as a breach of regulations.

7

Achieving the adoption order

This chapter sets out the legal effect of an adoption order, the law and procedures for achieving adoption orders, and the duties of adoption agencies and local authorities.

The legal effect of adoption orders

An adoption order transfers parental responsibility for the child from the birth parents and others who had parental responsibility, including the local authority, permanently and solely to the adopters. The child is no longer in care or looked after by a local authority. Any residence order, care order, freeing or placement order is discharged, and social workers have no right to visit or be involved in the family life of the child unless the family invite them to, apart from requesting information for reviews of support services. Adoptive families are however still entitled to an assessment of their adoption support needs after the adoption order has been granted.

The child is deemed in law to be the child of the adopters, as if they had been born to them. Their surname is usually changed to that of the adopters (unless the adopters choose not to) and their birth certificate is replaced by an adoption certificate that shows the adopters to be the child's parents. A child who is not already a British citizen acquires citizenship if adopted in the UK by a British citizen, or if adopted abroad under the Hague Convention by a British citizen. Finally, inheritance is from the adoptive family, not the birth family.

When an adoption order application can be made
The age of the child
A child or young person who is to be adopted must not be married or have entered into a registered civil partnership. They can be of any

nationality and must be 18 or under. The application for the adoption order must be made before the young person's 18th birthday.

Non-agency adoptions

Notification of intention to apply for an adoption order

Notice of intention to apply for an adoption order must be given in writing to the local authority where the prospective non-agency adopters live, no more than two years and at least three months before the application can be lodged with a court. (A Section 44 notice under ACA 2002)

Period of residence before the adoption order can be applied for

Stepparents - 6 months

The adoption order can be applied for after a child has lived with a stepparent for at least six months, provided the stepparent has given three months notice to their local authority before making the application.

Alternatives to adoption for married or civil registered stepparents

During the three month notice period the local authority may ask stepparents married to, or civil registered with the child's birth parent, to consider legal alternatives to adoption which allow these stepparents to share parental responsibility for the child by agreement with each of the birth parents with parental responsibility, or by granting parental responsibility orders (CA 1989, Section 4a).

These alternatives allow the stepparent to share parental responsibility and therefore make decisions about the child together with the birth parent. However, unlike adoption, the child's legal relationship with the birth parent they do not live with continues.

Even if stepparent applicants are not attracted to these alternatives, the social worker assessing their suitability to adopt, and considering the welfare of the child, will report their reasons for not choosing these alternatives to the court, which will take them into account. The court can decline to make the adoption order if it considers these alternatives to be better for the child.

Intercountry adopters - 6 months

Intercountry adopters can apply to adopt after the child has lived with them for six months if they have followed the correct legal procedures and regulations for intercountry adopters, e.g. have been approval by an agency before going abroad to collect the child, and must give notice to their local authority of the child's arrival in the UK, and their intention to apply for an adoption order within 14 days of the child entering the UK.

Foster carers wishing to adopt without the support of the child's local authority – one year

They can apply for an adoption order after the child has lived with them for at least one year immediately preceding the application, and have previously given three months notice to the local authority where they live, or can apply earlier if a court gives them permission.

Relatives – three years

Where a child has been placed for adoption by their parents with close relatives, an application for an adoption order can be made when the child has lived with the adopters for three years, and they have previously given three months notice to their local authority. They can apply earlier if a court gives them permission.

Private foster carers – three years

The application for an adoption order can be made after the child has lived with private foster carers for three years, and they have previously given three months notice to their local authority. They can apply earlier if a court gives permission.

The 'Annex A' report in non-agency adoptions

After non-agency adopters give notice of their intention to apply for an adoption order, a local authority social worker will visit and assess the prospective adopters' suitability to adopt that child.
The prospective adopters must give the social worker sufficient opportunities to observe the child with them in the home environment. The social worker will advise in the court report they prepare whether the potential adopters are suitable to adopt the child and whether adoption is in the best interests of the child. This report is confidential to the court but prospective adopters can ask the court to exercise its discretion to order that the content of it (or at least those parts that refer to themselves) to be disclosed to them.

The information required for the Annex A court report is set out in Appendix 4.

Agency adoptions

10 weeks residence required – no notification of intention needed

Agency adopters are not required to notify the child's agency or their own agency of their intention to apply for the order. However, no application can be made for an adoption order until the child has lived with agency adopters for at least 10 weeks.

Making the decision to apply

The legal effect of the application

When any application for an adoption order is lodged in a court, the legal entitlement of parents, guardians or the local authority to remove the child from the prospective adopters is suspended unless the courts give permission for removal, or there are serious concerns that the child is suffering or at risk of suffering significant harm.

Non-agency adoptions

Non-agency adopters can apply for the adoption order when they feel ready to do so (after the residence and notice periods set out above). If the parents or guardians are willing to give their consent to the order being made the application is likely to move forward smoothly.

However, sometimes non-agency adopters wish to progress the adoption order against the wishes of the parents or guardians, and local authority foster carers may want to adopt the child they are fostering without the support of the child's local authority. Potential adopters must then convince the court that it is in the best interests of the child to dispense with the parents' or guardians' consent to the making of the adoption order. In the case of foster carers adopting against the views of the local authority, they will also have to convince the court that the adoption order is in the best interests of the child despite those views. It is likely they will need expert legal advice to overcome such obstacles.

Agency adoptions – making the decision to apply for the adoption order

When all is going well in an agency adoptive placement, the decision to move forwards towards adoption will usually be reached by a consensus between the prospective adopters, the social workers, and the child (where they are of an age to understand). The decision to apply might be made at a review, but remains the decision of the prospective adopters. It is not made by the social workers, the reviewing officer, or the adoption panel, and their approval is not required in law.

If prospective adopters are not supported by the child's local authority in making the application, they may still apply, and the adoption order application will prevent the local authority from removing the child unless the court gives permission or there are serious concerns that the child is suffering or at risk of suffering significant harm.

Choosing the court to make the application

The court fee

This is £140 per child in all courts. Applicants in receipt of income support, tax credits or who have a very low income may not have to pay the court fee. If the application for an adoption order is supported by the child's local authority, it is expected that they will pay this fee as part of their adoption support services (chapter 5).

Non-agency adoptions – which court?

Where the consent of the parents or guardians to the making of the adoption order is likely to be given, and therefore the application is straightforward, the local Magistrates Court (the Family Proceedings Court) will usually be the best place to start the application. The court premises are usually more convenient to travel to than those of the County Court, and the hearing may be scheduled more quickly than in the County Court. An application to a County Court must be made to a County Court Adoption Centre.

Help with the application

Adoptive applicants are entitled to help from members of the court staff in the family office, who will, for example, provide information about court procedures, and copies of the application form. However, court officials are not allowed to give legal advice.

8

If the application for an adoption order is likely to be consented to by a child's parents or guardians the application will probably be straightforward, and legal advice may not be necessary. However, if in any doubt, non-agency adopters should consult a solicitor, Citizen's Advice Bureau, or a legal advice centre. Sometimes the assessing social worker may also be able to advise, but social workers are not legally qualified, and it might be prudent to check their advice.

If parents or guardians are not likely to consent, applicants should seek expert legal advice before making the application. Public funding (formerly called legal aid) to pay for advice and representation may be available to adoptive applicants on a very low income, but is not automatically available. Applicants for public funding will have to demonstrate not only their very low income, but that the application has 'merit', and has a reasonable chance of being successful. This is particularly relevant to some stepparent applicants whose could choose legal alternatives to adoption (see above).

Agency adoptions – which court?

1. The court nearest to the prospective adopters

Although this might seem the obvious first choice, the child's birth parents with parental responsibility will be notified of the application being made, and be told the date and court at which the application will be heard (see below). Therefore if prospective adopters do not wish their location to be disclosed to the birth parents, the court most local to their home might not be the wisest choice.

2. The court nearest to the child's placing local authority area

This may also be a suitable choice, as it may be the court that knows the child's circumstances because previous court proceedings were held there. It would also be convenient for the child's social worker, who needs to attend court for the adoption hearing.

However, because the courts must notify the child's birth parents or guardians of the making of the application (see above), a court near the birth parents' home and relatively easy for them to travel to, might also not be the wisest choice for agency adopters.

3. Magistrates Court or County Court?

Magistrates Courts have a great deal of experience in dealing with relatively straightforward non-agency adoption order applications, especially stepparent adoptions. The applications may be scheduled for hearing more quickly than in County Courts. However, County Courts have considerably more experience of contested or more complex adoptions, and those concerning looked after children. Therefore, prospective adopters of looked after children are advised to make their application for the adoption order to a County Court. If an application is made to the Magistrates Court which appears to be complex or likely to be heavily contested, it may be transferred to the County Court.

It should be possible to choose a County Court Adoption Centre (most of which are located in the middle of cities) that is relatively convenient for the prospective adopters, but will not reveal to the birth parents the location of the adoptive home. Before choosing the court, agency prospective adopters are advised to read the rest of this chapter, and take into account the advice of their social workers and/or solicitors, based on their knowledge about how well the courts known to them operate in terms of protecting adopters' confidentiality.

Help with the application
Where the decision to apply for an adoption order is made with the support of the social workers, agency prospective adopters are entitled to their help in making the application, helping with paperwork, and providing advice about procedures. The prospective adopters are also entitled to help from members of the court staff, such as information about procedures, and copies of the application form. However, court officials are not allowed to give legal advice.

Agency adopters will need their own independent solicitor if the adoption order application is opposed by the parents or guardians, if there are likely to be disputes about contact after adoption (see below), or the child is given their own legal representation. The child's local authority is expected under ASSR 2005 to meet the adopters' legal costs if it supports the adopters' application.

Agency adopters might wish to consult their own solicitors in any application, and should certainly do so if they intend to make an application against the views of the local authority. In these circumstances the local authority is very unlikely to assist the applicants with court fees or legal costs. A solicitor will advise about whether public funding will be available.

The application form

Agency and non-agency adoptions

The Application Form A58 must be completed by or on behalf of the adoptive applicants and signed and dated by them, and the original and three copies given to the court. Adopters should keep a copy for their own records. The form requires information about the adopters, the child and the child's parents or guardians. This information will include names and addresses, dates of birth when the children came to live with them and who was involved in arranging the adoption placement etc. Crucially, it will also include the legal circumstances of the child; whether the child was authorised to be placed for adoption by an agency, or if this is a non-agency adoption with or without parental consent etc. These circumstances will determine how the adoption order application proceeds.

Serial number to protect identities

If the applicants do not wish their identities or location to be known to the birth parents or guardians they can ask (on the application form) for the court to give them a 'serial number'. Once the court has issued a serial number, any documents sent to the parents or guardians of the child will contain this number rather than about the names and addresses of the applicants. In addition, when the applicants and the parents or guardians of the child attend the court hearings, the court will make arrangements to ensure that the applicants' identity remains protected.

Other documents to be provided to the court

All adoption order applications

The adoptive applicants must provide the following documents to the court with the application:

1. If the adopters are married or civil registered, the certified copy of their marriage or civil registration certificate. (This will be returned when the adoption order has been made)
2. A certified copy of the child's birth certificate, or if the child has previously been adopted, a certified copy of the entry in the Adopted Children Register.

3. If an adoptive applicant is a widow or widower, or the surviving partner of a registered civil partnership, a certified copy of the death certificate.

4. If adoptive applicants have been divorced or a civil partnership has been dissolved, a certified copy of the Decree Absolute or dissolution certificate.

Health reports for some non-agency adoptions

In non-agency adoptions, except adoptions by stepparents, medical reports are required on the applicants' health and the health of the child. These need to be made during the period of three months before the date of the application. No health report is needed with the adoption order application if the child is being adopted by a stepparent, or in agency adoptions.

Placement order or section 19 consent form – agency adoptions

If the child has been authorised to be placed for adoption by Section 19 consent or a placement order (chapter 3) the court must be given a 'sealed' copy of the placement order (i.e. with the court's stamp on it), or the original signed and witnessed Section 19 consent form. The order or consent form will be given by the witnessing CAFCASS officer to the child's local authority, and then to the prospective adopters.

The 'Annex A' Report - agency adoptions

The child's local authority is required to write an Annex A report for the court when agency adopters apply for an adoption order. This report sets out the local authority's view on whether the applicants are suitable to adopt the child and if adoption is in the child's best interests. This report is confidential but prospective adopters can ask the court to exercise its discretion to order disclosure of it (or those parts referring to themselves) to them. The information required for the Annex A Report is set out in Appendix 4.

Parental consent to the making of an adoption order

Non-agency adoptions

One of the questions on the application form is whether the applicants believe the child's parents or guardians are willing to consent to the making of the adoption order. If they are, the court will appoint an officer from CAFCASS to interview the parents or guardians. The officer will ascertain if they are giving their consent with full understanding of the legal consequences, and unconditionally, and if so, they will witness the parent's signature on the consent form, and tell the court that consent has been given. The original of the consent form will be forwarded to the adoption agency.

Parents or guardians living abroad

Where the parents or guardians are outside the UK, a CAFCASS officer in the UK is not required to check or witness their consent. Their consent should be witnessed either by a person authorised in that country to administer an oath for any judicial or other legal purpose, a British Consular Officer or Notary Public. If the consenting parent or guardian is serving in any of the regular armed services, an officer holding a commission in any of these services may also witness the consent being given.

Permission to oppose the adoption order – agency adoptions

A child is placed with agency adopters after authorisation by either Section 19 consent being given, or a placement order granted (chapter 3). If a placement order has been granted, or Section 19 consent has been given and not withdrawn before the adoption order is applied for, the parents or guardians may not oppose the adoption order being made unless the court gives them permission.

The court's permission to oppose the making of the adoption order may not be given easily. This is because the court which granted the placement order will have dispensed with parental or guardians' consent to placement for adoption, on the grounds either that the child has suffered or was at risk of suffering significant harm due to the standard of parental care, or the parent or guardian has previously consented to placement for adoption.

The criteria for being given permission to oppose is that there has been a "change in circumstances" since the placement order was granted, or Section 19 consent given, and the welfare of the child requires permission to be granted. There is an argument, if it is otherwise appropriate and in the interests of a child, for the adoption order application to be made as soon as possible after the tenth week of placement – before parents or guardians have had time to make the positive changes in their circumstances which might warrant them being given permission to oppose.

If permission to oppose is not given, the prospective adopters do not need to ask the court to dispense with the parents' or guardians' consent to the making of an adoption order. The only issues for the court then to consider will be whether granting an adoption order is in the best interests of the child and arrangements (if any) for contact after the adoption order (see below).

Implications for agency adopters

The small window of opportunity for parents and guardians to obtain the court's permission to oppose the making of an adoption order is potentially a source of great concern for future agency adopters. It is impossible to know at the early stage of the operation of the new law how many parents will obtain permission to oppose, or what impact this new law will have on recruitment of future adopters.

Permission to oppose may rarely be granted where the child has suffered significant harm in the parents' or guardians' care in the past, (as will be the case for most children placed by agencies) and/ or their reasons for wishing to oppose the adoption order are not centred on the child's welfare.

In most applications for adoption orders, agency adopters will have the combined help of the agency social workers, local authority lawyers, their own legal advisers and sometimes CAFCASS officers to work towards achieving the adoption order if it is right for the child. The court's decision about giving permission to oppose and whether the adoption order should be granted will depend ultimately on the child's welfare being the paramount concern.

Dispensing with parental consent

All adoptions

The Statement of Facts

If the parents or guardians have obtained the court's permission to oppose the application for a looked after child, or if non-agency adopters do not have the consent of each parent or guardian to the adoption order being made, the court must be asked to dispense with their consent. This is achieved by submitting to the court three copies of a Statement of Facts, along with the other documents. This document should be prepared and signed by a lawyer. It sets out the evidence for proving one of the three legal grounds for dispensing with parental consent.

These grounds are that either:

1. **The parents or guardians cannot be found**
   The applicants must provide via their solicitor evidence to the court of what efforts have been made to find them, and the court must be satisfied that all reasonable efforts and enquiries have been made.
2. **The parents or guardians are incapable of giving consent**
   This means that they are not legally competent because of illness or disability, and medical evidence will be needed to prove this.
3. **The welfare of the child requires that consent should be dispensed with**
   The court – assisted by the local authority and any CAFCASS officer appointed – will consider if adoption is in the child's best interests, taking into account the welfare checklist (chapter 3) and if so, will dispense with the parental or guardians' consent at the final hearing.

Implications for agency adopters

For the vast majority of agency adopters, the application for an adoption order will be successful, given that a court decided at the placement order stage that the child should be placed for adoption, and if the child is happy and having their needs met by the prospective adopters.

In these circumstances the court is very likely to consider the adoption order to be in the best interests of the child and if required to do so, dispense with parental consent.

Directions hearings about the application

These are relatively informal court hearings – usually taking place round a table in a room off the main court. The first directions hearing will usually be within four weeks of the application being lodged at court. The judge or magistrates will consider the proceedings and make decisions (known as 'directions') about procedural matters prior to the final hearing, including:

a. whether there are any errors or omissions in the application or documents that need to be corrected;

b. in non-agency adoptions, the need for the applicants to provide a statement explaining the background to the application, reasons for wishing to adopt, and any other relevant information.

c. tracing or notifying parents or others that the application has been made, if appropriate (see below).

d. the timetable for the social worker and any CAFCASS officers to provide their reports to the court and provide any other evidence.

d. whether any documents should be disclosed to the applicants or to the parents or guardians of the child.

e. whether the child should be made a party to the application.

f. whether the case should be transferred to another court.

g. whether a further directions hearing is necessary.

h. if possible, the date and place of the final hearing.

Adoptive applicants need not attend directions hearings personally, provided their legal representatives attend, and have taken instructions from the prospective adopters about the issues which might arise. Prospective adopters might ask their lawyer to raise at directions hearings the practical arrangements to be made by the court to ensure their identity is protected should the birth parents attend the court for the final hearing.

A copy of the court order explaining what directions have been made will be sent to the applicants or their solicitor. Once directions have been given, the court will monitor the progress of the application to make certain that the timetable and any directions are complied with.

Notification to birth parents and guardians of the application for an adoption order

In all adoptions (except where a freeing for adoption order was made), parents and guardians have parental responsibility for their children when adoption orders are applied for. The law requires that they are notified by the court when an adoption application is made, and must be told when and where the application will be heard. The only exception to this is parents who have given Section 20 consent to the making of an adoption order previously, and given notice that they do not wish to be informed of the application (see chapter 3). People who have Section 26 contact orders in their favour (chapter 6) will also need to be notified.

Attendance at court by parents and guardians

Parents or guardians, and those with Section 26 contact orders in their favour, are entitled to attend the final court hearing of the adoption order application (except those who have given section 20 notice) and be heard by the courts as to whether the order should be granted. They can also apply for contact orders (section 8, CA 1989) to be granted with the adoption order.

Implications for agency adopters

This is another potential source of anxiety for agency adoptive applicants and their social workers, and may influence the choice of court for the adoption order application (see above). However careful court staff and legal representatives are about arrangements in court buildings and at hearings – use of video conferencing facilities, separate entrances and appearances in the courtroom for parents and adopters etc – these may not prevent every unwanted or unplanned encounter between the prospective adopters and parents or guardians, around the court buildings.

In anticipation of the new law, plans have been drawn up by judges and court staff to try to avoid some of the potentially unhappy consequences of this new law – for prospective adopters who would usually need to attend court for the hearing of their application for an adoption order, but whose identity is to be kept confidential.

Attendance at the final court hearing by the adopters

The court rules allow the final hearing of the adoption order application (which birth parents will be entitled to attend) to be held without the prospective adopters and child present, but represented by lawyers. This may be the most effective way of avoiding the anxiety of an unwanted or risky encounter between adopters and birth family at court. However if the application is opposed, the court may be reluctant to allow the adopters to be absent, because of the necessity to ensure there is a fair hearing for all, including birth parents, by the prospective adopters being available to give evidence.

The adoption ceremony

If and when the decision is made by the court at the final hearing to grant the adoption order, the happy occasion on which the adoption order is pronounced to the adopters and child by the judge (the 'adoption ceremony') will be separated from this final hearing in time and perhaps date and place. The birth parents or guardians will not be notified of, or entitled to, attend this ceremony.

The impact of this new law will be monitored very closely during 2006, including looking at any evidence in support of amending it if it has led to frequent and distressing encounters at court.

Applications for contact orders to be made with the adoption order

Parents (both with and without parental responsibility), guardians and people with Section 26 contact orders in their favour at the time of the application for the adoption order, are entitled to ask the court to make Section 8, Children Act 1989 contact orders in their favour, or for support from the court for formal agreements for contact to be established (see chapter 6).

The court has a duty when considering making an adoption order to hear their views about what the contact arrangements should be after adoption, as well as the views of the adopters, the local authority for the child and any CAFCASS officer appointed to represent the child.

If a court is persuaded that an order for contact after adoption is in the best interests for a child, it can grant a Section 8 contact order with the adoption order, that adopters must comply with. It is not yet possible to know if many of these orders will be made under the new law; they were available but extremely rare under the previous law.

Implications for agency adopters

This is a third potential source of anxiety for agency adopters – that a court will impose contact orders on them which they do not feel comfortable with, or there will be an unpleasant dispute at the adoption hearing about what the contact arrangements should be. Case law (decisions made by courts in the past which influence current courts) demonstrates a reluctance by courts to impose contact orders on unwilling adopters. This may continue to happen under the new law, for children being adopted when continued contact by the birth family may not be in their best interests.

However at the point when an adoption order is about to be made there is an opportunity for careful consideration by prospective adopters of what is being said about the child's need for contact, and which arrangements (if any) might be best for them, both in the immediate and longer term future. It provides an opportunity for adopters, social workers, parents, guardians and CAFCASS officers to negotiate and agree (if necessary via legal representatives) contact arrangements to meet the needs of the child. Prospective adopters should take into account that well-negotiated fair and child-centred agreements are very likely to avoid contact orders being imposed and to be more sustainable and successful than contact orders.

Children as parties to adoption order applications

Court rules provide that in some circumstances children will be parties to adoption order applications. This means they will have their own solicitor to advocate their views to the court, and a CAFCASS officer will be appointed to advise the court about whether the adoption order (or any other order) is in the interests of the child. A child will be a party if:

1. The parents or guardians have been given permission to oppose the adoption order.
2. The child opposes the adoption order.
3. There are disputes about contact.
4. The child is being adopted by a relative.
5. A CAFCASS officer persuades the court that the child should be a party.
6. The child is to live abroad after the adoption.

The child's solicitor will be paid for from public funding.

Implications for adopters

The views and wishes of the child (and considerations as to their welfare) will be advocated to the court separately from the views and wishes of adoptive applicants, parents or guardians or anyone else who is a party to the application. Clearly, the implications for adoptive applicants will depend upon whether the child wants to be adopted, whether they want contact orders or arrangements to be made, and what is said on the child's behalf about their welfare.

If the child does not want to be adopted, wants contact arrangements or orders which their adopters are not comfortable with, or the court is persuaded that adoption is not in a child's best interests, the adoptive applicants will have to reconsider their position. They should take legal and social work advice about whether to pursue their application to adopt, consider alternative orders, or continue to contest the contact orders or agreements being requested.

Alternative court orders

A court considering whether to make an adoption order must also think about whether any other order (under ACA 2002 or CA 1989) or no order would be better for the child. These alternative orders may also be applied for by parents or guardians who have been given permission to oppose the making of adoption orders.
Alternative orders made in favour of the would-be adoptive applicants might be appropriate if, for example, an older child does not want to lose their identity as a child of the birth parents, or change their nationality, but needs the legal security of an order that allows them to remain with the adoptive parents.

Other possible orders (under the Children Act 1989) are:

Residence Order – Section 8
This determines that the child is to live with the holders of the residence order and gives the holders parental responsibility for as long as the order is in force. They therefore have the right, shared with parents or guardians, to make all other decisions about a child, except the right to consent or withhold consent to the child's placement for adoption, or the making of an adoption order, or

8

appoint a guardian for the child. The order finishes when a child reaches 16, unless the court specifies that it is to last until the child's 18th birthday.

A residence order also discharges a care order. The child cannot be known by a new surname or removed from the UK for more than one month without the leave of court, or the written permission of each parent or guardian with parental responsibility.

Unlike adoption, the legal identity of the child does not change, they remain the child of their birth parents, and their nationality and immigration status does not change. The birth parents remain liable for child support.

Special Guardianship Order – Section 14

This order is a 'halfway house' between a residence order and an adoption order. It gives parental responsibility to the special guardians, shared with the birth parents, but allows the special guardians to exercise parental responsibility to the exclusion of birth parents on most issues. This gives the special guardians the 'legal upper hand', rather than the equal sharing of parental responsibility with birth parents of a residence order.

A special guardianship order discharges a care order. Special guardians can appoint guardians for a child (to look after the child following their death) and (together with birth parents with parental responsibility) must give consent to the child's placement for adoption with other people, and can withdraw that consent. If given permission to oppose, their consent to the making of an adoption order to others must be dispensed with by a court (together with that of the birth parents with parental responsibility). The special guardianship order comes to an end when the child is an adult at 18 years old.

The special guardians cannot cause the child to be known by a new surname or removed from the UK for more than three months without the leave of court, or written permission of each parent with parental responsibility. Unlike adoption, neither the legal identity of the child (as the child of their birth parents) nor their nationality or immigration status changes. The birth parents remain liable for child support.

A special guardianship order is intended to be more permanent and legally secure than a residence order but less so than the adoption order. It will be harder for parents to discharge a special guardianship order than a residence order as they would need the permission of the court to apply. This would only be granted if there had been a significant change in circumstances since the order was granted and the welfare of the child requires permission to be given.

The adoption ceremony

All adoptions
When the court has decided at the final hearing that the adoption order should be granted, a date will be set for the meeting at court for the adoption order to be pronounced by the judge or magistrates to the child and their adopters (the 'adoption ceremony').

This happy occasion is arranged to be as informal as is possible within a court setting. If in the County Court, it is usually in a side room, rather than an actual court. The judge or the magistrates will be present, usually with their clerk to assist them, along with the social worker for the child, the adopters and the child.

Sometimes the judge or magistrates will ask questions of the adopters or the child, usually based on what they have read in the court papers about a child's hobby, favourite football team etc. Then the adoption order will be granted and in some courts, a 'child friendly' certificate of adoption will be given to them on the day. This is not the adoption order, which will be sent later by the court.

This adoption ceremony can be experienced by the adopters and child as very brief and something of an anticlimax after the worry and tension of the final hearing, although some courts do their best to bring a sense of occasion and even fun into it. Sometimes the judge or magistrates will invite photographs to be taken. The best part of adoption day is usually the party or other celebration afterwards!

The adoption order
Some weeks after the adoption ceremony a copy of the adoption order will be sent to the adopters from the General Register Office and their marriage or civil partnership certificate returned to them by

the court. In urgent cases, such a holiday planned for shortly after the adoption, the adoption clerk at the court may be able to provide a document to enable the adopters to get a passport for the child.

The adoption certificate

Adoption certificates (short and full versions) will be issued by the Registrar General and sent to the adopters. These replace the child's original birth certificate, and are in the adopted child's new name and with the adopters shown as the child's parents.

A short certificate carries no reference to adoption and is indistinguishable from any other short birth certificate showing date, place and country of birth, adoptive forename and surname, and gender. The short certificate can be used by an adopted person for most legal and administrative purposes in place of the original birth certificate. A full adoption certificate shows the name, surname and address and occupation of adoptive parents, the date of adoption order, and the name of the court.

8

If things go wrong – legal obligations, rights and remedies

This chapter applies specifically to agency adoptions. In previous chapters the possibility of something going wrong at various stages in the adoption process has been referred to, along with some ways to ensure problems do not happen. This can include making sure before placement that all the information about a child is accurate and current, that contact arrangements are understood and acceptable, and that the support services to be provided are adequate. This chapter describes how the law can help prospective adopters and adopters to seek solutions if problems occur, and what adoptive parents should know about their legal rights and obligations.

Adoption is a complex and lengthy process with many potential difficulties, some capable of legal remedy and others not. Before the adoption order the prospective adopters' social worker should be the first source of help if the family is running into difficulties. They should advise about how problems can be resolved or eased, and if necessary negotiate with the other agencies involved. Below are the most common difficulties, and their possible legal solutions.

Assessment and approval as adopters

The new law makes it possible for more people to be eligible to become adopters and chapter 3 set out the procedure for being approved as agency adopters. Nobody has a right to be assessed, but potential adopters do have a right to be prepared adequately for the task of adopting, and treated fairly and openly in the assessment and approval process. This includes the right (but not the obligation) to attend the panel considering their suitability to adopt. Prospective adopters also have the right to an independent review of their agency's proposal not to approve them or to terminate their approval. The IRM procedure has had a significant impact in achieving reconsideration of proposals not to approve. In first year, in each case where the IRM recommended approval the agency subsequently approved adopters they had originally proposed not to.

Prospective adopters are entitled to know most of what the agency holds on record about them, with some exceptions to protect the confidentiality of personal referees etc. Prospective adopters will know what is said about them in the Prospective Adopters Report at least working 10 days before the adoption panel, with the opportunity to correct any inaccuracies or misinterpretations.

Prospective adopters are in a good position to demand fair and open treatment by agencies if they know how the regulations and standards require agencies to undertake assessment and approval. If prospective adopters believe that their agency has been unfair, lacked openness or failed to meet their legal duties, they should first remind agencies of these obligations. If this does not solve the problems, and neither does the IRM, the three possible ways of redress are: using the agency's complaints procedure, taking the case to the Local Government Ombudsman, and bringing a judicial review (see below).

Foster carer adopters

Foster carers wanting to adopt, even those wishing to adopt against the views of the child's agency, have the same right to fair and open treatment as other prospective adopters, including an IRM review, if the agency assesses them as adopters. However they cannot insist on the child's agency assessing their suitability to adopt. As set out in chapter 8, they do not need that assessment or approval to apply for an adoption order when the child has lived with them for one year, although they must give three months' notice to the child's agency before making the application. However, going ahead without seeking prior approval may make it less likely that the foster carer adopters will receive favourable decisions about adoption support and may find their application to adopt opposed by parents and the local authority.

Review and termination of approval

Chapter 3 sets out the procedure for agencies to review the approval of their prospective adopters at least once a year, until a child is placed. Regulations require that this review should be carried out by a manager or social worker in the agency who did not undertake the original assessment.

The result of the review will usually be a continuation of the approval. If no placement has happened after one year of approval the agency should consider how the chances of the prospective adopters can be improved. However, if the agency wishes to terminate approval, it must prepare a Prospective Adopters Review Report and ask the adoption panel to make a recommendation. Prospective adopters receiving notification that the agency proposes to terminate their approval should see that report, have 10 working days to correct any errors or misinterpretations before the panel, and must be invited to attend the panel.

A review must also be undertaken if any additional information is received, or there are developments which throw doubt on the original approval, e.g. a disruption of a child's placement before the adoption order is granted. This is when the child returns to local authority care either at the adopters' request or if the local authority decides that the child should not live there anymore. Where there has been a disruption, prospective adopters should try to ensure that a disruption meeting is held before the prospective adopters' review is presented to panel (see below). Without an independently chaired and properly conducted disruption meeting, prospective adopters may be vulnerable to their review and presentation to the panel being unfairly influenced by the social workers involved in the disruption.

Information about a child

Chapter 3 explains how and when prospective adopters should receive information about a child offered to them, and Appendix 3 sets out the detailed content of the Child's Permanence Report. This report should be provided to prospective adopters at a very early stage, prior to their first meeting with the child's social worker.

The Child's Permanence Report must contain detailed and current information about the child, which should be sufficient to allow the prospective adopters to make an informed choice about whether the child offered is right for them. Regulations also provide that adopters can ask for, and must be provided with, more information.

9

In the recent past, courts have allowed adopters to sue local authorities when inadequate information was provided about a child and the adopters took on a child whose extreme behaviour caused great distress. This was when the law was less clear about what information should be provided and when. A claim for compensation is less likely to succeed now, unless it can be proved that the child's local authority failed to comply with regulations, concealed information or deliberately misled prospective adopters about a child.

Support services during placement

Chapter 5 sets out the legal obligations of the child's local authority to assess for, consult prospective adopters about, and provide a written plan for support services before a child is matched and placed. This gives prospective adopters the opportunity and right to ensure the support package is adequate before the child joins the family. If it is not, they may consider declining or delaying the placement.

Prospective adopters also have the right at any time during the placement and after the adoption order, to an assessment of their support needs. If an adoptive family needs help which was not anticipated at placement, or different types of support, they should make a written request for an assessment of their support needs. This must be undertaken by the child's local authority, or the local authority where the adoptive family lives. The request should be made through the local authority's ASSA. An extra copy of the request sent to the Director of Child and Family Services in the local authority might ensure it is not overlooked – especially if the ASSA cannot be identified. The regulations do not specify the time period in which the assessment must be completed, but the more urgent the need for support, the quicker the response should be. A delay of months, rather than weeks, unless there is a good reason, might warrant a complaint. A lack of staff to undertake the assessment is not a valid reason for delay, as local authorities can commission assessments by independent social workers, therapists, etc.

As chapter 5 sets out, local authorities have the discretion to decide whether to provide support services to an adoptive family following the assessment. However, their decisions must be reasonable and can be legally challenged if adopters feel they are not. If the support contained in the support plan is not provided, a request for assessment of support needs is not complied with, or assessed needs for support are not met, the prospective adopters' social worker might be able to resolve the problem by negotiation and advocating the prospective adopters' needs to the local authority.

Help from the Independent Reviewing Officer (IRO)

Support services to the adoptive family are part of the care plan for the child. During a placement IROs have a problem solving role (see chapter 7) as the people, independent of the local authority, who must focus on the child's needs and welfare and monitor the implementation of the care plan. IROs have a duty to attempt to resolve 'defects' in that implementation, including a lack of assessment for support needs, or unreasonable decisions not to provide support needs. IROs must therefore tackle the local authority.

Prospective adopters may consider asking their child's IRO to convene a review (in addition to those statutorily required) to bring people face to face in a meeting about support chaired by the IRO. This could be much more effective than phone calls and emails in bringing the problem and possible solutions to the attention of all concerned. If an IRO cannot resolve the problem within the local authority, they must consider referring the matter to CAFCASS (see chapter 7) so that their solicitors can consider taking legal action on behalf of the child.

Support after adoption

The duty to assess for support needs of an adoptive family continues after the adoption order is granted and so does the discretion to provide support services. Chapter 7 sets out which local authority is responsible after the adoption order is granted.

If local authorities are unable to provide support themselves, or lack the expertise (e.g. for therapy for a child) they must consider commissioning and funding outside organisations such as registered adoption support agencies to provide it on their behalf. Again, prospective adopters should be able to access help and support from the ASSA to ensure that the local authority explores these avenues.

There is the same obligation to respond within a reasonable time to a request for assessment after adoption as during adoptive placement. In addition decisions made about the provision or lack of provision of support services must be reasonable and are challengeable if they are not by the local authority's complaints procedure, Local Government Ombudsman and judicial review as set out below. Prospective adopters might also be able to bring to the attention of the child's local authority their failings in respect of support by the timing of their application for the adoption order (see below).

Contact during adoptive placement

Chapter 6 sets out the law in relation to contact and adoption, along with the implications for adopters. Prospective adopters should have been given sufficient written information, and been consulted about contact arrangements planned for a child during the adoptive placement and after adoption. There should have been consensus about the arrangements and what is expected of the prospective adopters. If the prospective adopters are not comfortable with the proposals for contact they may have to consider postponing or even declining the placement. However in making that decision should listen very carefully to what is being said about the needs of the child and take advice from their social worker and/or the child's.

If Section 26 orders have been made before or during the adoptive placement prospective adopters must comply with these. If no section 26 contact orders have been made or no written agreements about contact have been entered into by the prospective adopters during placement planning, they are not obliged to follow 'instructions' about contact issued by social workers, CAFCASS officers or IROs.

If Section 26 contact orders or agreements about contact are not working in the best interests of the child, they can be changed. Contact agreements can be renegotiated with the assistance of social workers and/or mediators. They can also be changed by an application to court to end (revoke) or change (vary) the order. The child's local authority, the child, their birth parents and close relatives can apply for a Section 26 contact order, or to revoke or vary an existing order, without seeking the court's permission first. Prospective adopters need the court's permission to apply for Section 26 orders. If the prospective adopters and the child's local authority agree that an order should be made or changed, it would be reasonable to expect the local authority to take the necessary legal action. If the child's local authority and the prospective adopters do not agree, the prospective adopters should consider taking legal advice about making an application, or ask the child's IRO to consider facilitating legal action by the child. (See below and chapter 7).

Help from the Independent Reviewing Officer

Contact arrangements during an adoptive placement are part of the care plan for the child, and IROs have a problem solving role (set out in chapter 7) and must focus on the child's needs and welfare and monitor the implementation of the care plan. IROs therefore have a duty to attempt to resolve 'defects' in that implementation, including contact arrangements (too much, too little, the wrong kind) which are adverse to the child's welfare or their stability in the adoptive home. Prospective adopters might consider asking the IRO for their child to convene a review in addition to those statutorily required, to bring the people face to face in a meeting about contact chaired by the IRO.

Contact after adoption

Chapters 6 and 8 set out how Section 8 contact orders can be made with adoption orders or after adoption orders have been granted, although they have only very rarely been made under the old law. Adopters may also enter into agreements to provide contact at the same time as the adoption order is made. Contact orders must be complied with, and so must agreements. If they are not, the people to whom the contact orders have been granted or with whom agreements have been made may be given permission to apply to court for an order under Section 8 to replace the agreement, or bring measures to enforce the Section 8 order.

Under previous law it was very rare for courts to give permission to anyone to apply for a contact order after the adoption order has been made. It remains to be seen whether it will be as rare under the new law, and adopters will need expert legal advice if permission is given.

The application for an adoption order

Chapter 8 sets out when and how the application for the adoption order can be made, and the legal effect of the adoption order. Normally a consensus is reached during adoptive placements about the right time to make the application. However the decision to apply (or not) is the legal right of the prospective adopters once the tenth week of a placement has been reached.

9

Some prospective adopters will be very keen to proceed as soon as possible for all the right reasons. In some cases there will be pressure to apply by social workers, CAFCASS officers or IROs which may or may not be for the right reasons (perhaps in an attempt to bring the local authority's or IRO's obligations to an end as soon as possible). At other times prospective adopters might be advised to consider applying for the adoption order earlier than they might otherwise want to do, to avoid the child being removed against their wishes.

This may be when there is a dispute between the prospective adopters and the child's local authority about contact, support or other matters. Some prospective adopters who have made complaints about the services received from the local authority run the risk of being perceived by that authority as troublesome or unpleasant to work with. In this context, it is not uncommon for social workers to believe the child should no longer be placed with those prospective adopters, and consider their removal. The only legal way for the prospective adopters to get swift relief from the anxiety this generates, and to prevent removal, is to apply for the adoption order.

The legal effect of making the application is that the child's local authority cannot remove the child unless a court gives them permission, or they have serious concerns that the child is suffering or is at risk of suffering significant harm.

Disruptions of placement

'Disruption' is used to describe a placement which has not achieved its desired time span. Most adoptive placements are successful, but sadly some are not and result in either the prospective adopters asking for the child to be returned to the care of their local authority or child's local authority deciding the placement should end.

Child's legal circumstances after a pre-adoption order disruption

Reviews

The child is still looked after by the local authority and subject to a placement order (or possibly Section 19 consent) and regulations require that a statutory review of the child should be held no sooner than 28 days and no later than 42 days after the disruption. This review should consider the future plans for the child; specifically, whether adoption is still the right care plan for the child.

The prospective adopters may be invited to this review, but cannot insist on attending because they will have lost parental responsibility for the child. However good practice would require them to be invited to contribute their views on what happened during the placement and what might be best for the child in future. This review of the child is not a 'disruption meeting', which serves a different purpose.

Disruption meetings and support after disrupted placements

Where a placement ends, regardless of the circumstances, there is a need for intensive support for both the child and the prospective adopters because the disruption will have left people involved feeling upset, angry and guilty. Support after disruption is one of the support services which local authorities must provide to adoptive families generally.

Although not a legal requirement, it is considered essential that the child's local authority convenes a disruption meeting, to which the prospective adopters are invited. This meeting considers both the factors which led to the placement breaking down, and information which might help determine the best way forward for the child and the prospective adopters. If the child's agency declines to convene a disruption meeting the prospective adopters might consider making a complaint. The disruption meeting could be vital to the successful outcome of the prospective adopters' review and continued approval.

Whilst disruption meetings are inevitably painful, especially for the prospective adopters, they are helpful in moving towards healing the hurt, anger and guilt which may be experienced. The disruption should be examined in a way which is intended to address the problems, not apportion blame, and constructively plan for the child's future. This is an opportunity for the prospective adopters to make their points about how the actions or inaction of their social worker or the child's may have contributed to the disruption. These may include that support was never provided, contact arrangements were not conducive to the child settling in the placement, or there was a lack of vital information etc. However, prospective adopters should also be prepared to consider if and how their own actions, attitudes and possible mismatches between their expectations and the reality of adoption may have been factors in the disruption.

9

Independent chairing of disruption meetings

Disruption meetings should be chaired independently of the agencies involved by a social worker qualified and experienced in adoption practice. The meeting will include discussion of:

a) The whole of the child's life, including what happened to them in their original family, the reasons for becoming looked after, and their experiences whilst being looked after.

b) The assessment process for the prospective adopters.

c) The selection process that led to the child and the prospective adopters being matched.

d) The process of introductions.

e) The placement.

f) The disruption and subsequent actions.

g) Conclusions and recommendations.

Disruptions after the adoption order

Sadly some children leave their adoptive homes and return to being looked after by the local authority after they have been adopted. This can be much later, including in the difficult adolescent years. Support after disruption is one of the range of services which local authorities must provide to adoptive families generally. If adopters would welcome help from the agency in coping with the distress of a disruption, and in understanding the factors which led to it, and this support is not offered, they may consider exercising their right to an assessment of their support needs from their agency (see chapter 5).

Child's legal circumstances and making decisions about them

After the adoption order, adoptive parents have sole parental responsibility for their child, and it is only ended by granting an adoption order to other people, or the child becoming an adult. If the child leaves at the request of the adoptive parents, or their own request, they will be accommodated by the local authority under Section 20 of the CA 1989. The local authority does not have parental responsibility for them until a care order is granted (see below).

In these circumstances the adopters are still entitled to make decisions about the child, to have contact with the child, to refuse contact for their child with others, and to demand that the child is returned to them if they wish it. However adopters must take into account the increasing right of a young person as they get older to make their own decisions, and the legal obligation of local authorities

9

to make plans for young people whom they are looking after, even without having parental responsibility, to promote their welfare and education. Young people also have the right to ask for and be given some medical treatment and advice (e.g. about contraception or abortion) without their parents being told or giving consent.

If the adopters do not want the child returned to them they must consider whether continuing to insist on their legal right to make decisions for the child in a future not shared with them is in the child's best interests, or whether 'loosening the reins' of decision making and delegating them to the local authority and the young person would be better in the short and long term. An example might be where the child is placed in foster care after the disruption some distance from the adoptive home and their school place needs to be changed, to avoid a lot of travelling, and to allow the young person to make new friends near their current home. The temptation to hang on to decision making for a child or young person who is not returning to the adoptive home may hamper the planning for the their future to the extent that it becomes harmful. In extreme cases, the local authority may be able to convince a court that a care order is justified.

Care orders for adopted children

If there are child protection issues about an adopted child (actual or risk of significant harm attributable to the adopters), or the child is 'beyond the control' of their adoptive parents, the local authority may have grounds to apply for an interim care order or emergency protection order. If granted by a court these orders give the local authority the legal entitlement to remove a child against the wishes of the adopters. If care proceedings are started by the local authority the adopters (as the child's legal parents) have a right to public funding to pay for advice and representation in court by a solicitor. If a care order is granted the adopters will share parental responsibility for the child with the local authority, but the local authority will have the legal upper hand and be able to make many decisions about the child in spite of the views of the adopters.

Reviews of looked after children following disruption

As adopters hold parental responsibility for their child they are entitled to participate in statutory reviews of their child, to be consulted on their views concerning their child and to attend the reviews, unless the IRO decides that their attendance at some parts of a review is not in the child's interests. It might be, for example, that the young person does not wish to meet them at the review, in which case the IRO should arrange for the review to include periods where the young person attends without their adoptive parents. As legal parents the IRO cannot refuse the adopters an opportunity to attend some part of the review unless there is a very unusual reason such as significant risk from them to other people.

If the placement disrupted before the adoption order, the prospective adopters do not have the same legal entitlement to insist on attending reviews as they do not have parental responsibility after the placement ends. However, because of their recent and close involvement as carers for the child they should probably be considered by the IRO as appropriate or relevant persons who should be consulted about their wishes and feelings concerning the child. They should therefore attend at least part of the review (if they wish) unless there are reasons why this is not in the child's best interests, or the child does not wish to meet them at the review.

Parents might also want to send their own written reports to reviews (if these are not requested) to ensure that their views are recorded, rather than relying on someone else's interpretation of their views.

Parental financial contributions for looked after children

As the legal parents of the adopted child or young person, whether they are accommodated or subject to a care order, adopters have the legal obligation to maintain their looked after child financially. Local authorities are entitled under the Children Act 1989 to recover financial contributions for looked after children under 16 years old unless the parents are in receipt of income support or tax credits.

They must first send a written notice to the parents specifying the weekly sum the local authority considers should be paid by the parents and the arrangements for payment. These arrangements include the date on which the obligation to make payments begins (this must be a date after the date of the notice), when it is to end, and when the first payment is to be made.

The local authority may not specify a weekly sum greater than it would pay to foster carers of a similar child, or it is reasonably practical for the parents to pay in their financial position. Therefore parents do not need to begin payments until they have received this written notice, and they have reached an agreement with the local authority about what is reasonable. They can challenge the amount specified if they do not think it is reasonable. However, if agreement cannot be reached the local authority could ask a court to grant a contribution order, which the parents would have to comply with.

Making complaints

Every adoption agency must have a complaints procedure, which should be publicly known, and the procedure for making complaints must be made available to a complainant.
In addition local authorities have a specific duty under the Children Act 1989 and the 2006 Representations Regulations (see Appendix 1), to consider complaints and representations concerning looked after children, and services provided to adopters. The complaints might concern any of the matters referred to in this book including contact, support services, assessment and approval, etc.

The complaints manager
Each local authority must appoint a complaints manager and ensure that everyone involved in the handling of complaints, including independent persons, is familiar with the complaints procedure.

Providing information about the procedure
When a local authority receives complaints, they must send the complainant as soon as possible an explanation of the procedure set out in the regulations, and either offer assistance and guidance on the use of the procedure, or give advice on where they may obtain it.

Where oral complaints are made, the authority must record them in writing, and send them to the complainant, who shall be given the opportunity to agree that they are accurately recorded in writing.

Implications for adopters

Prospective adopters or adopters should make sure the local authority understands that if they make an oral complaint (for example at a review or on the telephone) the local authority officer

> hearing it is told that this is a complaint. This triggers their
> duty to record it and start the complaints procedure. However
> complainants are advised to also put their complaints in writing.

Informal resolution of complaints – 'Stage 1'

Many local authorities attempt to resolve complaints initially by
suggesting a consideration of them within the local authority service
complained about – often by the persons who made the decisions
complained about, to try resolve the matter quickly without the
involvement of outsiders. This is a 'stage 1 complaint' and the local
authority must consider and try to resolve the complaint within
10 working days. Experience suggests that stage 1 complaints are
not always dealt with quickly and are rarely successful when the
complaints are of the serious nature referred to here, and where
other ways of trying to resolve the problems have already been tried
and failed. However, if adopters think the problems may be helped
by an internal consideration they might give the local authority the
opportunity to offer a solution this way, provided it is addressed
within the required 10 days.

'Stage 2'

If the complaint cannot be settled by 'stage 1' or the complainant does
not want it considered internally and informally, the local authority
must appoint an independent person to take part in a more formal
consideration of the complaint. The local authority must investigate
the complaints with the independent person and formulate a response
within 25 days of receiving them from the complainant. If the local
authority cannot comply with this time limit they must, within the
25 days, tell the complainant in writing why not; and give a date, no
later than 65 days from the start date, when they will have concluded
their consideration and send their response.

It is not however the independent person who undertakes ('considers')
the investigation of the complaint. The person undertaking the
investigation is usually another officer of the local authority, although
they must work with the independent person, who will check their
work. Some local authorities commission people from outside their
employment to investigate the complaint, but for the purposes of the
task they are employed by the local authority and their independence
cannot be guaranteed, except by scrutiny by the independent person.

The independent person must take part in any discussions which are held by the local authority about the action (if any) to be taken in the light of their consideration of the complaints.

Implications for adopters

It can easily be seen that the complaints procedure at 'stage 2' does not guarantee that adopters will have a fair chance of their complaints being properly investigated with a sufficient degree of independence or objectivity. It also cannot be guaranteed that complaints will be investigated and resolved within the 25 day deadline, and the experience of Adoption UK members is that (with some exceptions) the worse the treatment by the local authority originally complained about the less likely it will be resolved promptly or to their satisfaction at 'stage 2'.

The complaints review panel - 'Stage 3'

The complaints procedure provides a 'stage 3' panel which must be appointed by the local authority (in England) to review the complaint if the complainant informs the authority in writing within 20 days that they are dissatisfied with the proposed result at 'stage 2', and want the matter to be referred to a panel. Under regulations in force in England from 1 September 2006, all three panel members must be independent (the equivalent Welsh regulations require a panel independent of the local authority). The panel must meet within 30 working days of receiving the complainant's request.

The complainants are entitled to attend the panel meeting and can be accompanied to the meeting by another person of their choice, who may speak on their behalf. At that meeting the panel must consider any oral or written submissions from the complainant or the local authority; and the independent person. Within 5 working days of the meeting the panel must send its report to the local authority, the complainant, and the independent person. Within 15 working days of receiving the panel's recommendations the local authority must send the complainant its response and proposals, along with information about making a complaint to the Local Government Ombudsman.

Recommendations

A panel must decide their recommendations and record them with their reasons in writing within 24 hours of the meeting. The panel must provide their recommendations to the local authority, the complainant, the previous independent person and any other person whom the local authority considers has sufficient interest in the case.

The local authority must, together with the independent person appointed to the panel, consider what action (if any) should be taken in relation to the child in the light of the complaint, and the independent person must take part in decisions about that action.

Implications for adopters

It is easy to see that the 'stage 3' panel of a complaint made by adopters is also not guaranteed to produce the desired result – although the experience of adopters is that sometimes it does. It is certainly worth trying – especially with the tighter and more definite timetables set by the 2006 regulations, and the new requirement that all panel members be independent.

Adopters attending these panels should be very well prepared with the points they want to make and the evidence in support of them available in written form to submit to the panel and to help them when speaking. If someone (who could be a lawyer) is to speak on their behalf, the adopters should keep a careful record of the evidence and points presented by the local authority complained about during the hearing.

Local Government Ombudsman

If adopters and prospective adopters are unhappy about how the local authority has dealt with them or the services offered to them they must use the local authority complaints procedure first.
If this is not successful in resolving complaints or moving things forward positively, or adopters believe the local authority has not addressed their complaints fully or properly, they can complain to the Local Government Ombudsman. The Ombudsman will normally only consider a complaint after the local authority's complaints procedure has been tried, i.e. the council has had the chance to answer the complaint.

The Ombudsman looks for 'maladministration' by a local authority that has caused an individual 'injustice'. This is something that the local authority has done wrong, or failed to do, that directly affected adopters and prospective adopters. One example is injustice caused by not getting a service they were entitled to, or there was an unreasonable delay in getting it. Another is if the local authority's actions or inactions have caused distress, inconvenience or uncertainty.

The Ombudsman will investigate the complaint until they achieve a fair result with the local authority. The Ombudsman makes recommendations to the local authority as to how a fair result can be achieved. These may include compensation, reconsideration of a decision not taken properly initially, or improvements to the local authority's procedures so that similar problems do not occur again. A complaint should be made to the Ombudsman within 12 months of first knowing about the matter complained about.

Implications for adopters

The services of the Ombudsman are free and readily accessible to adopters and prospective adopters who have tried unsuccessfully to resolve problems through the local authority complaints procedure. Whilst this service is therefore only available at the end of months or years of struggling with the local authority, the very clear and well protected independence of the Ombudsman, and the quality and thoroughness of their investigations, gives considerable hope to adopters. The Ombudsman has dealt with numerous complaints in recent years by adopters and foster carers given a poor service by local authorities, and the end result has been positive for most.

Judicial review

If a complaint to the local authority and the Local Government Ombudsman has been unsuccessful, a last option is to apply for a Judicial Review by the High Court. Professional legal advice is essential in pursuing this course of action. Judicial review is a court proceeding where a High Court judge considers the lawfulness of a decision or action by a public body, such as a local authority –including whether it was a 'reasonable' decision.

The judge looks at how the decision was taken. As a result the court may decide that the decision (for example, on whether to provide adoption support services) was taken in the wrong way, but it will then not substitute a different decision. Instead, it is likely to ask the local authority to make the decision again. This may lead to the local authority making the same decision, but in the right manner, or it may make a different decision.

The court will look at the local authority's decision on these grounds:
1. Illegality – does the local authority actually have the legal power to make this decision?
2. Irrationality – was the decision so unreasonable as to be "perverse" or "irrational"?
3. Unfairness – was the decision-making process fair? E.g. was there a fair hearing, was the process biased, or was there an abuse of power?
If the judicial review succeeds, the court can make either a:
1. Quashing order – overturns the decision and the public body must take the decision again in a proper fashion.
2. Prohibiting order – stops the body from taking an unlawful decision or action.
3. Mandatory order – requires the body to carry out a specific action in reaching its decision, e.g. consult with the appropriate people.
4. Declaration – states what the law is or what rights the parties have, but does not make an order.
5. Injunction – prevents an illegal act being performed or ensures that a duty is performed.
6. Damages – awards monetary compensation where human rights have been infringed.

There are strict time limits for applying for judicial review. A claim must be made within three months of the conclusion of unsuccessful complaints to the local authority and the Local Government Ombudsman.

Implications for adopters

A judicial review action can be very expensive, depending on how far the case goes and for most people public funding and assistance to pay the legal costs will not be available. Judicial review is a last resort that may be appropriate in a handful of cases. However legal advice should be taken promptly, and in some cases when the local authority is warned by the legal representative of the possibility of a judicial review, things which have not been decided previously may suddenly reach resolution.

Access to information about adoptions and intermediary services

One of the biggest changes in adoption law and practice concerns access to information about adoptions – both past and present – for adopted adults and their birth relatives, and how people who access the information are entitled to help in achieving contact and reunion by professional intermediary agencies.

This chapter sets out how these changes may affect adoptive families and their adopted children as adults, and describes the safeguards in the law against the possibility of contact from birth family members which may not be welcome. There are different regulations and guidance depending on whether adoption orders were granted before 30 December 2005 ("pre-commencement adoptions") or on or after 30 December 2005 ("post-commencement adoptions").

Pre-commencement adoptions

The law

The Adoption Information and Intermediary Services (Pre-Commencement Adoptions) Regulations 2005 (SI No 890) in England, and the Adoption Information and Intermediary Services (Pre-Commencement Adoption (Wales) Regulations 2005 (SI No 2701) in Wales (hereafter both referred to as ISR 2005) provide procedures for adults adopted before 30 December 2005 to obtain information about their adoption and make available a route for contact between adopted adults and their adult birth family members. There is also statutory guidance for agencies about how to operate this new law, which must be followed unless there are exceptional reasons not to.

The regulations set out a framework which enables intermediary agencies to operate a service to assist in arranging contact between adopted adults and their adult birth relatives. As an independent third party, the intermediary agency seeks information from a range of sources to help them trace either adopted adults or adult birth relatives and – subject to obtaining their informed consent – disclose identifying information about them to the person requesting the service. They can then facilitate contact or the exchange of information, depending upon what both parties want. Counselling and support to deal with the issues raised may also be provided.

Who can apply for an intermediary service?

Adopted adults and their adult birth relatives both have the right to apply for an intermediary service, although there is no right to have the service provided. Each group has different issues. For instance, most birth relatives have little information to use to try to trace their adult adopted relatives. Adopted adults however, have a long established right to information about their adoption and family history. Schedule 2 to ACA 2002 provides that, on reaching the age of 18, an adopted person can apply to the Registrar General for the information needed to obtain a copy of their original birth certificate. Adopted adults may also apply to the agency who arranged their adoption for access to their birth records. This is likely to include identifying information about their birth parents and sometimes others involved in their adoption.

Under the Adoption Agencies Regulations 1983, adoption agencies can disclose information they consider appropriate to an adopted person. Most adopted people apply for information first before deciding if they want to pursue contact with a birth relative. Some adopted people will want to undertake their own research to establish the identity and whereabouts of their birth family. They may then ask an intermediary agency to make the initial approach to the birth relatives. In other cases, the intermediary agency may undertake the research and tracing on behalf of the adopted person, or the adopted adult may approach the birth relatives directly themselves – this has been the usual way in the past of renewing contact with their birth family.

With the wider availability of intermediary services, adopted adults (and adoptive parents supporting them) should consider the benefits of using an intermediary service. There are many advantages to having an independent, experienced and trained third party acting as a 'go-between' in what can be an intensive and emotionally draining

10

journey. An intermediary service will help manage the exchange of information and any reunions, as well as providing support and advice. There is likely to be a charge for this service, but a skilled intermediary will increase the chances of a successful reunion.

Priority

The new law takes into account how adoption was managed in earlier times. Before the mid-1970s, adoption was mostly of children born to unmarried mothers, when single parenthood was viewed by society as shameful. Many women were 'sent away' with the birth concealed from friends and family, and the child placed for adoption with little involvement or choice for their mothers. It was usually arranged that there would be no contact between the birth parents and the adoptive family. The new law acknowledges the needs of such birth parents for information about and potential reunion with their adopted adults.

Therefore, the regulations for pre-commencement adoptions make a distinction between adoptions before and after 12 November 1975 (ISR 2005, Regulation 5(2) England and Wales). In England, intermediary agencies must prioritise applications for information about adoptions before 12 November 1975. This is because many of the birth parents involved will now be elderly or have life shortening conditions. In Wales, agencies simply must prioritise applications before that date.

10

Implications for adopters

This information is important for adoptive parents, especially as from the 1970s onwards adoption became more about children being adopted from the public care system as a result of child protection concerns. It is likely that in the immediate future intermediary services will concentrate on adoptions before 12 November 1975. The adopted adults here will be at least 30 years old, and so have reached maturity, which may give some reassurance for adoptive parents concerned about the possible effects on them and their family of an approach from a birth family member.

However, intermediary agencies can accept applications in relation to adoptions granted after 12 November 1975 if they believe the circumstances are sufficiently exceptional, for example where the applicant is terminally ill. Furthermore, an agency with spare capacity (except in Wales), does not need to prioritise pre 12 November 1975 applications. It is hard to know how this aspect of the regulations will work in practice and whether adoptive families will be able to enforce the spirit of the regulations and guidance.

Provision of intermediary services

Intermediary services can only be provided by local authorities or voluntary adoption agencies, or adoption support agencies. These are a new type of organisation created by ACA 2002, which must be registered with the Commission for Social Care Inspection and are subject to regulation and inspection. Their conditions of registration must specify that they provide intermediary services.

There is no legal duty for all adoption agencies to provide an intermediary service. They are not providing intermediary services where they are just providing information to an adopted person about their adoption, so an adopted person only seeking such information should continue to apply to the agency which holds the case records. If they then wish to explore contact with their birth family they will need to approach an intermediary agency, if the adoption agency that holds their records does not provide intermediary services.

A person adopted before 30 December 2005 may apply to the Registrar General for information needed to obtain a copy of their original birth certificate (under ACA 2002, Schedule 2). That information can then be used to undertake a search for a birth relative using public records.

An intermediary service is required to:
- Undertake preparatory work with the applicant.
- Obtain information (e.g. from adoption agency records, court records and the Adopted Children and Adoption Contact Registers).
- Use that information to trace and contact individuals.
- Act as an intermediary between the applicant and the subject and facilitate contact.
- Provide counselling, support and advice.

Approaches from birth family members

Adopters may be concerned about approaches from birth family members. Both the birth relative and the adopted person must be

18 before an application can be initiated (ISR 2005, Regulation 5(3) England and Wales).

In addition, an intermediary agency has a discretion not to proceed with any request for a service, "where it would not be appropriate to do so" (ISR 2005, Regulation 6(1) England and Wales). In making this decision, the agency must take into account:

- The welfare of the applicant (the birth relative), the subject (the adopted adult) and any other persons who may be identified or affected by the application (including adoptive parents and the adopted person's siblings, and the wider family).
- Any views of the appropriate adoption agency (i.e. the agency that arranged the adoption or that holds the adoption records).
- Any veto recorded.
- Any information obtained from the Adoption Contact Register.
- All the other circumstances of the case.

In particular, the agency must have regard to the welfare of any person under the age of 18 who may be identified or affected by the application. So, if the adopted adult has a younger sibling, the intermediary agency must consider carefully what affect the birth relative's approach may have on that sibling.

10

The Statutory Guidance (Paragraph 38) makes it clear, that: "although the agency is not routinely required to seek the view of the adoptive parents, it will need to exercise its discretion as to whether it is appropriate to do so, having regard to the particular circumstances of the case". Paragraph 39 states: "The views of the adoptive parents will not on their own be decisive but one of a range of factors to which the agency must have regard in deciding whether to proceed, or continue proceeding, with the application."

In deciding to provide an intermediary service, agencies will have to consider the information they hold (if they are the appropriate adoption agency) and may need to gather additional information from the Adoption Contact Register. Where the intermediary agency is not the appropriate adoption agency, it will need to contact the appropriate agency and ascertain its views on the application and any proposed contact.

Implications for adopted persons and adoptive parents

When a birth relative requests an intermediary service, the decision by an agency on whether or not to proceed with the application is a key one for adoptive families. Initially that decision is made without the knowledge of the adoptive family. Some adopted persons and their families may have no or only slight concerns about an approaches from birth relatives. Others may have serious concerns, perhaps related to the adopted person's past experiences, such as the abuse that led to their adoption. There may be other complications, such as disagreement between adoptive parents and adopted persons about how to handle any approaches. Adoptive parents may find it hard to accept that the ultimate decision is for the adopted adult to make. However, adoptive parents can play a crucial role in supporting their adult children in understanding what is involved and reaching a decision that is in their best interests.

There are numerous factors to consider. The immediate reaction may be to think that approaches from the birth family will always be from birth parents. However, approaches may also be from siblings, half-siblings, aunts, uncles, grandparents etc, which may be more acceptable.

Approaches from a birth family member via an intermediary service do not always mean that contact and reunion will follow. Whatever happens should be the decision of the adopted adult, who could decide not to proceed with any approach, either initially or permanently, or agree only to the exchange of information. Depending on the outcome of this exchange, contact might then never happen, happen immediately or happen in the future.

What can adopters/adopted persons do if they are concerned about an approach?

There are various safeguards for adopted adults and/or their parents who do not want to be approached by the birth family (ISR 2005).

Registering a wish

Where an adopted adult doesn't want contact with birth relatives, they can register this wish formally with the Adoption Contact Register. Until 30 December 2005, the Register was for those who wanted contact. Now adopted adults can specify those birth relatives with whom they do or do not wish to have contact.

Veto

Intermediary agencies must take into account any information on the Register in deciding whether to proceed with an application. However information on the Register is not an absolute veto to stop an application. It will be possible for intermediary agencies to discover a wish for no contact on the Register, but to proceed with the application.

Adopted adults may also formally register an absolute or qualified veto with the appropriate adoption agency (ISR 2005, Regulation 8 England and Wales). Such a veto will carry significantly more weight than any wish on the Adoption Contact Register.

An absolute veto prevents an intermediary agency from making an approach in any circumstances, while a qualified veto enables an agency to make an approach on behalf of a birth relative specified by the adopted adult or in circumstances specified by the adopted adult (e.g. information about a hereditary medical condition).

In registering a formal veto, the adoption agency must ensure that it is an "informed veto"; that the adopted person fully understands the implications, particularly where an absolute veto is being registered. Once the veto is registered, the adopted person can amend or withdraw it at any time. The veto continues until it is amended or retracted by the adopted person.

Although an absolute veto will prevent an intermediary agency from making an approach, there may be exceptional circumstances where the adoption agency considers it appropriate to pass on certain information, despite the veto. This might be where the birth relative making the application has information about a possible hereditary medical condition. In making the decision, the adoption agency has to

10

be fully satisfied that the circumstances are sufficiently exceptional to warrant contacting the adopted person to pass on this information.

There may also be some cases where birth relatives have established the identity or whereabouts of an adopted adult without using an intermediary agency. They may then apply to an intermediary agency, but an absolute or qualified veto may be in place that prevents the application proceeding. Given that the birth relative already has the information to make a direct approach, the adoption agency may decide to contact the adopted person to tell them this. The advice should state the veto would need to be amended or withdrawn to allow the intermediary service to proceed and to provide any necessary counselling and support. However, the agency should stress that if the veto is not amended or withdrawn, then the birth relative may choose to make a direct approach, outside the agency's control.

The adoption agency must keep a written record of any veto on the adopted person's case record. When contacted by an intermediary service for views on an application, the adoption agency must notify them of the terms and content of the veto.

Adoptive parents' views

The law recognises the need for intermediary agencies to consider how adoptive parents might be affected by an application. Whilst there is no legal requirement to find out adoptive parents' views on all applications received, they will often have invaluable information about their adult children, particularly in relation to any emotional, behavioural or developmental difficulties which need to be taken into account when considering the application. Adopters of physically or mentally disabled adults adopted children will be able to advise about the possible effects of an approach and their ability to deal with it.

Given this, adoptive parents may wish to write to the appropriate adoption agency to register their views on any future approach from an intermediary agency, whether such an approach may be well received or if they have any particular concerns. Adoptive parents should try to provide a balanced, objective view on the possible effects of any approach on their adult adopted children. It will be important to provide evidence, wherever possible, of the potential consequences of an approach. Such evidence might relate to any difficulties the child/adult has experienced, their mental capacity, the circumstances of the adoption, the contact history between the birth and adoptive families, the effect on siblings or other family members, etc. Adoptive parents should supply this information on or after their child's 18th birthday, to ensure that is given full consideration in any future application. Parents can provide information before their child is 18 years old, but it will not carry the same weight. (See also below.)

Views expressed before ACA 2002 came into force

Adoptive families should be aware that any views expressed to or recorded by the appropriate adoption agency, before 30 December 2005 will not constitute a formal veto. An intermediary agency will have to take these views into account, but they will not carry the same definitive weight as a formal veto. Adopted persons and their parents should register their views again, as a formal veto if necessary, with their adoption agency after 30 December 2005.

Consent to disclosure

Intermediary agencies cannot disclose identifying information to birth relatives about adopted adults without having first obtained the adopted adult's consent. (Identifying information is "information which, whether taken on its own or together with other information possessed by the applicant, enables the subject to be identified or traced" (ISR 2005, Regulation 7(4) England and Wales).)

This is an important safeguard for adopted adults; the right to decide whether to encourage or reject an approach from a birth relative via an intermediary. The adopted adult will decide what, if any, identifying information should be released to the birth relative. For those concerned about approaches from birth relatives, registering a veto with the appropriate adoption agency will be the clearest expression of consent, particularly where the adopted person's consent is not a simple "yes" or "no" to every approach.

The regulations also cover difficult situations, such as where the adopted adult has died or lacks the mental capacity to give informed consent. Where the adopted person has died, the agency has the discretion to disclose identifying information about them, having first taken into account the welfare of any other person who may be identified by disclosing the information or anyone else who may be

10

affected. The guidance (Paragraph 48) states that the intermediary agency should, "as a minimum, take steps to seek the views of the deceased person's next of kin before deciding whether it is appropriate to disclose the identifying information".

Where the adopted person lacks the mental capacity to give informed consent, the agency must also take into account the welfare of others who may be affected by the decision to disclose identifying information and may need to seek their views.

In seeking consent, the intermediary agency must take "all reasonable steps" to ensure that consent is an informed decision, by providing the adopted adult with information about the application and the background to the case (ISR 2005, Regulation 7(3) in England, Regulation 7(2) in Wales). It can also provide them with information about the birth relative, their circumstances and the reasons for their application. This may include information which identifies the birth relative, as the adopted person will wish to know who is making contact and their reasons for doing so.

Obtaining consent should be handled carefully and sensitively by the intermediary agency and it should advise the adopted person about available counselling services or other specialist support or advice.

Where consent is refused

If the adopted person refuses to give consent to the disclosure of identifying information, the intermediary agency has discretion to disclose non-identifying information to the birth relative if it considers it appropriate (ISR 2005, Regulation 9 England and Wales). This can include information such as the adopted person's family or domestic circumstances, their general health and well-being or other information which may be of comfort or value to the birth relative.

Counselling

The intermediary agency must provide the adopted person with written information about the availability of counselling and any fees involved. If they request counselling, the intermediary agency must secure its provision. The intermediary agency can charge the adoptee for these services. However:

"Where the subject (an adopted adult in this instance) has requested that counselling and support be provided, it is envisaged that any fees for counselling would normally be met by the applicant as it would not be appropriate to charge the subject in connection with a service they did not initiate. (Statutory Guidance Paragraph 109)"

In some cases, it may also be appropriate to request an assessment of the adopted adult's or adoptive parents' need for adoption support services.

Post-commencement adoptions

The law

For adoptions on or after 30 December 2005, the legal framework governing the management and disclosure of information is set out in Sections 56–65 of ACA 2002 and in the Disclosure of Adoption Information (Post-Commencement Adoptions) Regulations 2005 (SI No 888) in England, and the Access to Information (Post-Commencement Adoptions) (Wales) Regulations 2005 (SI 2689) in Wales (both referred to as AIR 2005). They specify the information adoption agencies must keep about a person's adoption, how long they must keep it, the information that agencies must disclose to an adopted adult on request, and the information that agencies may disclose to adopted people, birth relatives and others who apply.

10

Adopted persons

People adopted on or after 30 December 2005 must apply in writing to the appropriate adoption agency (i.e. either the agency which arranged the adoption or that holds their records) for the information needed to obtain a copy of their birth certificate. They should provide the following with their application:
- Current (and any previous) forename and surname.
- Name on adoption (if different from current name).
- Date of birth.
- Full names of adoptive parents.
- Name at birth/prior to adoption (if known).
- Date of adoption (if known).

If an adopted person applies to the appropriate agency, but it does not hold the relevant information, the agency must apply to the Registrar General for this information and then pass it onto the adopted adult, subject to an important caveat.

In certain circumstances, the agency can decide to withhold a copy of the birth certificate, and must apply to the High Court for an order denying the adopted person access to this information. An order will only be granted if the court is satisfied that there are exceptional circumstances, such as the agency having grounds to believe that disclosure could place others at risk of harm. The Statutory Guidance gives the example of a child being placed for adoption because of abuse by a birth family member and where the agency believes that disclosure could place birth family members at risk of serious harm.

Adopted adults can also receive from the agency the information given to their adopted parents before placement; i.e. the Child's Permanence Report. This will include identifying information about the child, their birth family and others, along with details of the child's early family life and history, their social, emotional development, health etc.

Agencies will need to consider carefully how best to disclose this information, as it could be upsetting or distressing. Agencies should consider providing the appropriate counselling and support during the disclosure process (Guidance Paragraph 6).

Adopted adults also now have the right to receive from the court which made the adoption order copies of documents relating to their adoption, including the application form for an adoption order, the adoption order and reports made to the court by a children's guardian or the adoption agency. However, the court can edit these documents to remove information defined as "protected" (see below).

Section 56 information

This is the information that adoption agencies must keep in their case records of children and adopters, and includes:
- The information on the adopted person's case record, including information about them as a child, their birth family, adoptive

parents and other persons involved in the adoption, such as former carers or social workers.
- Information given to the agency by the birth family (or other significant people in the child's life), along with other information that the agency may have obtained from the Registrar General and any other information which would enable the adopted adult to obtain a copy of their birth certificate. It also includes any information entered on the Adoption Contact Register.

This information can include identifying information and background information. Identifying information is any information held by the agency which, whether taken on its own or together with other information disclosed by the agency, identifies a person or enables them to be identified. This is defined as protected information and certain rules apply to its disclosure.

Protected information

The adoption agency can only disclose protected information in certain circumstances (set out in sections 60–62 of ACA 2002). Anyone is allowed to apply to an adoption agency for the disclosure of protected information about any person involved in an adoption. The procedures the agency must follow vary depending upon whether the information is about an adult or a child.

Adults

Where the application concerns protected information about adults, the agency does not have to proceed with the application, unless it considers it appropriate to do so, for example, where the disclosure may not be appropriate if it might be harmful to the welfare of the adopted person. If the agency decides not to proceed with the application, the applicant may seek a review of the agency's decision by an independent review panel.

If the agency decides to proceed, it must take all reasonable steps to obtain the views of the subject of the information, about its disclosure. Having received those views, or tried to obtain them, the agency may disclose the information if considers it is appropriate to do so. In doing this, the agency must consider:
- The welfare of the adopted person.
- The views of the person to whom the information relates.
- All the other circumstances of the case.

This gives the agency a wide discretion. It can even decide to withhold the information, contrary to the views expressed by the person the information is about. However, in such cases, the subject of the information may seek an independent review of the disclosure determination (see below).

In essence, if adopted people or adoptive parents apply for identifying or protected information about the birth family, the agency will need to seek the views of the birth family before deciding whether to release that information. Similarly, where birth family members apply for information about the adoptive family, the agency should contact the adoptive family to seek their views before deciding whether to disclose the information. In either situation, the adoptive family may apply for an independent review of the decision if they dispute it.

Children

In relation to protected information about children, the agency again has discretion not to proceed with an application for disclosure of information, unless it considers it appropriate to do so. Where it decides to proceed with the application, it must take all reasonable steps to obtain the views of any parent (including the adoptive parent) or guardian of the child, and the child (if the agency considers it appropriate, taking into account their age and understanding).

In taking any decision the adopted child's welfare must be the agency's paramount consideration (ACA 2002, section 62(6)). With any other child, the agency must have "particular regard" to their welfare.

Although the agency has discretion to disclose protected information in relation to a child, its discretion is more limited than in relation to an adult. Protected information will only normally be disclosed where the agency is satisfied that it is in the interests of the child's welfare to do so. To reflect this, there is no right to apply for an independent review of the agency's disclosure determination in relation to a child.

The disclosure of sensitive information can raise many issues, particularly where trauma and family disruption have been involved. Counselling can help families come to terms with the information disclosed. Although there is no requirement to undergo counselling, adoption agencies must provide information about counselling in relation to the disclosure of information. The agency must also provide that counselling or secure the provision of it where it has been requested. The agency can charge fees in connection both with disclosing information and providing counselling, but it cannot charge an adopted person for the reasonable costs incurred in processing an application for the disclosure of information.

Agreements to disclose protected information

In some situations, a formal written agreement may be made between the agency, birth parents and adoptive parents, or other adults (e.g. former carers or social workers) about the disclosure of protected information, where it is considered to be beneficial to the adopted child's welfare. Such agreements are likely to be rare, as the majority of children placed for adoption will have been subject to care proceedings and there may be some hostility from the birth parents towards the plan for adoption, and a need to maintain the confidentiality of the adoptive placement. However, where arrangements are formally agreed it will overcome the restrictions on disclosure of protected information set out earlier and release the agency from its duties to seek a person's views about disclosure.

The agreement can be in one of two forms. First, it can be a bilateral agreement between the agency and anyone aged over 18 about disclosing information in relation to that person (e.g. former foster carer, etc). The adult will have registered their views on the disclosure and so the agency will not to have to seek their views repeatedly.

Secondly, the agreement can relate to sharing protected information that is considered by the agency to be in the interests of the child's welfare. The agency, the adoptive parents and each person who, before the adoption order was made, had parental responsibility for the adopted person, may all be involved in this type of agreement.

The agency must keep a written record of any agreement, containing:
- The full names and signatures of the persons involved in the agreement.
- The date on which it was made.
- The reasons for making the agreement.
- Details of information that may be disclosed.
- Any restrictions on how the information may be disclosed.

10

Independent review

In England, where adopted persons or adopters challenge an agency's decision to disclose information (a "qualifying disclosure determination") they can apply for an independent review of that determination. Qualifying determinations include:

* Not to proceed with an application from any person for the disclosure of protected information.
* To disclose protected information contrary to the view expressed by the person the information is about.
* Not to disclose protected information about a person to the applicant where that person has expressed the view that the information should be disclosed.

An application for independent review must be made to the Independent Review Mechanism within 40 working days of the date on which the agency's written notification was sent. When informed that an application has been received, the agency must forward specified information to the independent review panel.

The panel is not an appeal process, but will review from an independent position the qualifying determination, and provide the agency with a recommendation about its decision to disclose or withhold protected information. The agency must then take into account the panel's recommendation before reaching a final decision.

Wales

In Wales, there is no provision for an independent review process. Where adopted people or adoptive parents wish to challenge any decisions, they will have to use the local authority or voluntary adoption agency's complaints procedure.

Appendix 1 – The legislation

Law is always subject to change by amending Acts, Regulations, and case law (the interpretation of legislation by the courts). All references in the text are to English regulations and guidance. Wales has its own secondary legislation.

Acts of Parliament (Statutes)

The main statutes for England and Wales referred to in this book are:

The Adoption and Children Act 2002

The principal statute governing the law of adoption, provides that the welfare of the child is the paramount consideration in making decisions about a child's adoption. The Act modernises and reforms adoption law, replacing the Adoption Act 1976.

The Children Act 1989

Governs the law concerning the care of children and covers both 'private' family law – arrangements about children between individuals within families, e.g. contact and residence orders- and 'public' family law, when local authorities provide services for 'children in need' living in their families or intervene in family life to protect children (care orders, emergency protection orders etc).

The Human Rights Act 1998

Gives effect in the UK to rights and freedoms guaranteed under the European Convention on Human Rights. All British courts and public bodies must make decisions in compliance with convention rights – the two most relevant to child care and adoption law are Articles 8 (right to privacy of family life) and 6 (right to a fair trial).

The Care Standards Act 2000

Provides for the Commission for Social Care Inspection in England (CSCI) and the National Assembly in Wales, to be responsible for the registration and inspection of children's homes, adoption agencies and independent fostering agencies, and the inspection of local authority adoption and fostering services.

The Civil Partnership Act 2004

Enables same-sex couples to obtain legal recognition of their relationship by registering a civil partnership – the equivalent of marriage. The Act amends the Children Act 1989 and the Adoption and Children Act 2002 to provide civil registered couples with the same entitlement to acquire parental responsibility for children as married couples, where one is birth parent.

The Local Authority Social Services Act 1970 (as amended by the NHS and Community Care Act 1990)

Requires local authorities to establish a procedure for considering any representations (including any complaints) which are made to them in relation to the discharge of, or any failure to discharge, any of their social services functions in respect of individuals whom the local authority have a power or a duty to provide services to.

Regulations and Court Rules (Statutory Instruments)

These set out the detail of applying and using legislation. The most significant are listed below, and are referred to in the text.

Court rules

These provide the rules, procedures and forms for applications to the courts under the Children Act 1989 and Adoption and Children Act 2002:

The Family Procedure (Adoption) Rules (2005) SI 2795 [L. 22]
Covers applications ACA 2002 orders in every level of court.
Magistrates' Courts Family Proceedings Courts (Children Act) Rules 1991 SI 1991/1395 and County and High Court Family Proceedings Rules 1991 SI 1991/1247
Covers applications for CA 1989 orders (amended in 2005 to include special guardianship orders).

Regulations

Adoption services

The Local Authority Adoption Service [England] Regulations 2003 SI 370
Require that each local authority providing an adoption service must have a statement of purpose that sets out the aims and objectives of the service, and a children's guide. The service must be run in a manner is consistent with the statement of purpose.

Also include sections covering the persons managing the service, and about the conduct of the service, arrangements for the protection of children, staffing and fitness of workers, fitness of premises and complaints procedures.

The Voluntary Adoption Agencies and the Adoption Agencies (Miscellaneous Amendments) Regulations 2003 SI 367

Require voluntary adoption agencies to have a statement of purpose setting out their aims and objectives. This must be kept under review, and the agency must be run in a manner consistent with the statement. They also require a manager to be appointed for the agency and any branches. Provision is made for the fitness of the manager and branch manager, and requirements are imposed regarding the proper conduct of a voluntary adoption agency, and the need for appropriate training. They make further provision about the conduct of a voluntary adoption agency, in particular as to the protection of children complaints, staffing, and record keeping.

Adoption Agencies Regulations 2005 SI 389 (for England) Adoption Agencies (Wales) Regulations 2005 SI 1313

Govern how adoption agencies and their adoption panels are required to carry out their functions under the ACA 2002, including preparation and approval of prospective adopters, consideration of whether children should be placed for adoption, matching prospective adopters with children and supervision and review of adoptive placements.

The Restriction on the Preparation of Adoption Reports Regulations 2005 SI 1711

Apply to England and Wales, and place restrictions on the persons who may prepare reports about; the suitability of a child for adoption, the suitability of a person to adopt, and the adoption or placement for adoption of a child, in both domestic and intercountry adoptions.

The Suitability of Adopters Regulations 2005 SI 1712

Apply in England, and prescribe the matters to be taken into account by an adoption agency in determining, or making any report in respect of, the suitability of a person to adopt a child. They require the agency to have proper regard to the need for stability and permanence in a prospective adoptive couple's relationship, when determining their suitability. The Welsh provisions are in the Welsh Adoption Agencies Regulations 2005.

Adoption support

The Adoption Support Services Regulations 2005 SI 691
The Adoption Support Services (Local Authorities) (Wales) Regulations 2005 SI 1512 (W.116)
The Local Authority Adoption Service (England) Regulations 2003 as amended in 2005 by The Local Authority Adoption Service (England) (Amendment) Regulations 2005, SI 2005/3339

Make provision for local authorities to provide adoption support services for adoptive families as part of the adoption service maintained by them under the Adoption and Children Act 2002.

Access to information about adoptions

The most significant change here for adopters is that the birth family adults as well as adopted adults have the right to ask for an intermediary service etc.

The Disclosure of Adoption Information (Post-Commencement Adoptions) Regulations 2005 SI 888

Govern how adoption agencies keep information about each adoption and deal with applications for disclosure of this information for persons adopted on or after 30 December 2005.

The Adoption Information and Intermediary Services (Pre-Commencement Adoptions) Regulations 2005 SI 890

These make provision under section 98 of the Adoption and Children Act 2002 to assist persons adopted before 30 December 2005 to obtain information about their adoption and to facilitate contact between those persons and their birth relatives.

The Adopted Children and Adoption Contact Registers Regulations 2005 SI 924

Govern the Adopted Children Register and the Adoption Contact Register maintained by the Registrar General, including obtaining of information from the register and on the connection between this register and birth records.

Intercountry adoption

The Intercountry Adoption (Hague Convention) Regulations 2003 SI 118

Implement the 1993 Hague Convention on the Protection of Children and Cooperation in Respect of Intercountry Adoption.

The Adoptions with a Foreign Element Regulations 2005 SI 392

Apply to England and Wales and make provision relating to intercountry adoptions under the Adoption (Intercountry Aspects) Act 1999 and the Adoption and Children Act 2002.

Fostering

The Fostering Services Regulations 2002 SI 257 for England Fostering Services (Wales) Regulations 2003 SI 237 (W. 35)

Govern the approval and review of foster carers by local authorities, voluntary organisations, and independent fostering agencies, including establishing fostering panels, agencies' duties to children in foster homes and to foster carers, including foster care and foster placement agreements.

Special Guardianship
The Special Guardianship Regulations 2005 SI 1109
The Special Guardianship (Wales) Regulations 2005 SI 1513 (W.117)
Govern special guardianship orders provided for in sections 14A -14C Children Act 1989, and special guardianship support services.

Complaints by children, relatives and carers
The Children Act 1989 Representations Procedure (England) Regulations 2006 SI 1738
The Representations Procedure (Children) (Wales) Regulations 2005 SI 3365 (W.262)
Set out the procedure to be used by local authorities in dealing with complaints and representations about their services to children.

The Advocacy Services and Representations Procedure (Children) Amendments Regulations 2004 SI 719
Impose a duty on local authorities to provide advocacy services for children wishing to make complaints under the Children Act 1989 representations procedure. Section 26A requires local authorities to make arrangements to provide of assistance including by way of representation, to care leavers and children who make or intend to make complaints under sections 24D and 26 (3) of the Children Act 1989.

Reviews of children looked after by local authorities
Review of Children's Cases Regulations 1991 SI 895
The Arrangements for Placement of Children (General) Regulations and the Review of Children's Cases (Amendment) (Wales) Regulations 2002 SI 3013 (W.285)
Review of Children's Cases Regulations (Amendments) (England) Regulations 2004 SI 1419
The Review of Children's Cases (Amendment) (Wales) Regulations 2004 SI 1449 (W 149)
Govern how local authorities and voluntary organisations review cases of children they are looking after. Impose obligations on the 'responsible' authority to appoint an IRO with the review of each case of a child looked after or for whom accommodation is being provided, or who is authorised to be placed for adoption. Also require the local authority to inform the

IRO about any significant change of circumstances following a review or a significant failure to implement decisions made as a result of a review.

Adoption Agencies Regulations 2005 SI 389

Govern the timing and content of reviews of children authorised to be placed for adoption and in adoptive placements.

Guidance

Statutory Guidance

Statutory Guidance is issued under section 7 of the Local Authorities and Social Services Act 1970. It does not have the full force of law, but must be complied with by local authorities and other adoption agencies unless circumstances indicate exceptional reasons to justify a variation.

Adoption Guidance 2005 provides guidance for adoption agencies to the Adoption and Children Act 2002 and the Regulations and Court Rules, including the Adoption Support Regulations 2005.

Special Guardianship Guidance provides statutory guidance for local authorities to the special guardianship provisions in the Children Act 1989, and support services.

National Minimum Standards for Adoption Support Services set out guidance for the operation of adoption support services.

Independent Reviewing Officers Guidance provides statutory guidance for the role and functions of IROs for looked after children, including those authorised for, and placed for adoption.

National Minimum Standards for Adoption Agencies (local authorities and registered adoption agencies) set out the minimum requirements for the management, conduct and qualifications of staff for registered adoption agencies. An addendum to these was published in December 2005, and is applicable to voluntary adoption agencies in England and Wales and local authority adoption services in England. It imposes additional standards to regulate adoption agencies which provide adoption support services in England and Wales, that focus on achieving good quality service provision for adoptive children, adopted adults and their adoptive and birth families.

Practice Guidance

Practice Guidance sets out suggestions for good practice, which local authorities and voluntary agencies are expected to follow, and which will be relevant to their inspection and registration. Details of regulations and guidance are available from the Department for Education and Skills (www.dfes.gov.uk). Details of Welsh regulations and guidance are available from the National Assembly for Wales (www.wales.gov.uk).

Appendix 2

The information about prospective adopters which agencies must obtain

Schedule 4, Part 1, Adoption Agencies Regulations 2005

The agency must see documentary evidence of all the following information.

1. Name, sex, date and place of birth and address including the local authority area.
2. A photograph and physical description.
3. Whether the prospective adopter is domiciled or habitually resident in the British Islands and if habitually resident for how long.
4. Racial origin and cultural and linguistic background.
5. Religious persuasion.
6. Relationship (if any) to the child.
7. Description of the prospective adopter's personality and interests.
8. If the prospective adopter is married or has formed a civil partnership and is applying alone for an assessment of their suitability to adopt, the reasons for this.
9. Details of any previous family court proceedings in which the prospective adopter has been involved.
10. Names and addresses of three referees who will give personal references on the prospective adopter, not more than one of whom may be a relative.
11. Name and address of the prospective adopter's medical practitioner.
12. If the prospective adopter is:
    (a) married, the date and place of marriage;
    (b) has formed a civil partnership, the date and place of registration of that partnership; or
    (c) has a partner, details of that relationship.
13. Details of any previous marriage, civil partnership or relationship.
14. A family tree with details of the prospective adopter, their siblings and any children of the prospective adopter, with their ages (or ages at death).
15. A chronology of the prospective adopter from birth.
16. The observations of the prospective adopter about their own experience of being parented and how this has influenced them.
17. Details of any experience the prospective adopter has had of caring for children (including as a parent, stepparent, foster parent, childminder or prospective adopter) and an assessment of their ability in this respect.

18. Any other information which indicates how the prospective adopter and anybody else living in their household is likely to relate to a child placed for adoption with the prospective adopter.

Wider family

19. A description of the wider family of the prospective adopter and their role and importance to the prospective adopter, and their likely role and importance to a child placed for adoption with the prospective adopter.

Information about the home etc of the prospective adopter

20. Information about the prospective adopter's home and the neighbourhood in which they lives.

21. Details of other members of the prospective adopter's household (including any children of the prospective adopter whether or not resident in the household).

22. Information about the local community of the prospective adopter, including the degree of the family's integration with its peer groups, friendships and social networks.

Education and employment

23. Details of the prospective adopter's educational history and attainments and their views about how this has influenced them.

24. Details of their employment history and the observations of the prospective adopter about how this has influenced them.

25. The current employment of the prospective adopter and their views about achieving a balance between employment and child care.

Income

26. Details of the prospective adopter's income and expenditure.

Other information

27. Information about the prospective adopter's capacity to:

(a) provide for a child's needs, particularly emotional and behavioural development needs;

(b) share a child's history and associated emotional issues; and

(c) understand and support a child through possible feelings of loss and trauma.

28. The prospective adopter's:

    (a) reasons for wishing to adopt a child;

    (b) views and feelings about adoption and its significance;

    (c) views about their parenting capacity;

    (d) views about parental responsibility and what it means;

    (e) views about a suitable home environment for a child;

    (f) views about the importance and value of education;

(g) views and feelings about the importance of a child's religious and cultural upbringing; and

(h) views and feelings about contact.

29. The views of other members of the prospective adopter's household and wider family in relation to adoption.

30. Any other relevant information which might assist the adoption panel or the adoption agency.

Part 2 Regulation 25(3)(a)
Report on the health of the prospective adopter

1. Name, date of birth, sex, weight and height.

2. A family health history of the parents, any brothers and sisters and the children of the prospective adopter, with details of any serious physical or mental illness and hereditary disease or disorder.

3. Infertility or reasons for deciding not to have children (if applicable).

4. Past health history, including details of any serious physical or mental illness, disability, accident, hospital admission or attendance at an out-patient department, and in each case any treatment given.

5. Obstetric history (if applicable).

6. Details of any present illness, including treatment and prognosis.

7. Details of any consumption of alcohol that may give cause for concern or whether the prospective adopter smokes or uses habit-forming drugs.

8. Any other relevant information which the adoption agency considers may assist the adoption panel and the adoption agency.

Appendix 3

The content of the Child's Permanence Report
Information about the child

1. Name, sex, date and place of birth and address, including local authority.

2. A photograph and physical description.

3. Nationality.

4. Racial origin and cultural and linguistic background.

5. Religious persuasion (including details of baptism, confirmation or equivalent ceremonies).

6. Whether the child is looked after or is provided with accommodation under section 59(1) of the 1989 Act.

7. Details of any order made by a court with respect to the child under the 1989 Act including the name of the court, the order made and the date on which the order was made.

8. Whether the child has any rights to, or interest in, property or any claim to damages under the Fatal Accidents Act 1976 or otherwise which they stand to retain or lose if they are adopted.

9. A chronology of the child's care since birth.

10. A description of the child's personality, their social development and their emotional and behavioural development.

11. Whether the child has any difficulties with activities such as feeding, washing and dressing themselves.

12. The educational history of the child including:

(a) the names, addresses and types of nurseries or schools attended with dates;

(b) a summary of their progress and attainments;

(c) whether they are subject to a statement of special educational needs under the Education Act 1996;

(d) any special needs they have in relation to learning; and

(e) where they are looked after, details of their personal education plan prepared by the local authority.

13. Information about:

(a) the child's relationship with:

(i) their parent or guardian;

(ii) any brothers or sisters or other relatives they may have; and

(iii) any other person the agency considers relevant;

(b) the likelihood of any such relationship continuing and the value to the child of its doing so; and

(c) the ability and willingness of the child's parent or guardian or any other person the agency considers relevant, to provide the child with a secure environment in which they can develop, and otherwise to meet their needs.

14. The current arrangements for and the type of contact between the child's parent or guardian or other person with parental responsibility for them, their father, and any relative, friend or other person.

15. A description of the child's interests, likes and dislikes.

16. Any other relevant information which might assist the adoption panel and the adoption agency.

17. In this part "parent" includes the child's father whether or not he has parental responsibility for the child.

18. A summary, written by the agency's medical adviser, of the state of the child's health, their health history and any need for health care which might arise in the future.

19. The wishes and feelings of the child regarding the possibility of placement for adoption with a new family and their adoption, their

religious and cultural upbringing, contact with their parent or guardian or other relative or with any other person the agency considers relevant.

20. The wishes and feelings of the child's parent or guardian, regarding the child's placement of the child for adoption, including any wishes and feelings about the child's religious and cultural upbringing.

21. The agency's views about the child's need for contact with their parent or guardian or other persons the agency considers relevant and the arrangements the agency proposes to make for allowing any person contact with the child.

22. An assessment of the child's emotional and behavioural development and any related needs.

23. An assessment of the parenting capacity of the child's parent or guardian.

24. A chronology of the decisions and actions taken by the agency in the child's case.

25. An analysis of the options for the future care of the child which have been considered by the agency and why placement for adoption is considered the preferred option.

26. Any other information which the agency considers relevant.

Information about the child's family and others

Information about each parent of the child:

1. Name, sex, date and place of birth and address including the local authority area.

2. A photograph, if available, and physical description.

3. Nationality.

4. Racial origin and cultural and linguistic background.

5. Religious persuasion.

6. A description of their personality and interests.

Information about the child's brothers and sisters:

7. Name, sex, and date and place of birth.

8. A photograph, if available, and physical description.

9. Nationality.

10. Address, if appropriate.

11. If the brother or sister is under the age of 18:

(a) where and with whom he or she is living;

(b) whether he or she is looked after or is provided with accommodation under section 59(1) of the 1989 Act;

(c) details of any court order made with respect to him or her under the 1989 Act, including the name of the court, the order made, and the date on which the order was made; and

(d) whether he or she is also being considered for adoption.

Information about the child's other relatives and any other person the agency considers relevant:

12. Name, sex and date and place of birth.
13. Nationality.
14. Address, if appropriate.

Family history and relationships:

15. Whether the child's parents were married to each other at the time of the child's birth (or have subsequently married) and if so, the date and place of marriage and whether they are divorced or separated.
16. Where the child's parents are not married, whether the father has parental responsibility for the child and if so how it was acquired.
17. If the identity or whereabouts of the child's father are not known, the information about him that has been ascertained and from whom, and the steps that have been taken to establish paternity.
18. Where the child's parents have been previously married or formed a civil partnership, the date of the marriage or, as the case may be, the date and place of registration of the civil partnership.
19. So far as is possible, a family tree with details of the child's grandparents, parents and aunts and uncles with their age (or ages at death).
20. Where it is reasonably practicable, a chronology of each of the child's parents from birth.
21. The observations of the child's parents about their own experiences of being parented and how this has influenced them.
22. The past and present relationship of the child's parents.
23. Details of the wider family and their role and importance to:
    (a) the child's parents; and
    (b) any brothers or sisters of the child.

Other information about each parent of the child:

24. Information about their home and the neighbourhood in which they live.
25. Details of their educational history.
26. Details of their employment history.
27. Information about the parenting capacity of the child's parents, particularly their ability and willingness to parent the child.
28. Any other relevant information which might assist the adoption panel and the adoption agency.

Appendix 4

Annex A Court Report by the local authority when an adoption order is applied for

Section B: The child and birth family
Part 1 - Information
(i) The Child

- Name, sex, date and place of birth and address including local authority. NB: address of the child and local authority area will be supplied to the court on a separate document with the application.
- Photograph and physical description.
- Nationality.
- Racial origin and cultural and linguistic background.
- Religious persuasion (including details of baptism, confirmation or equivalent ceremonies).
- Details of any siblings, half-siblings and step-siblings, including dates of birth.
- Whether the child is looked after by a local authority. a) Whether the child has been placed for adoption with the prospective adopter by a UK adoption agency.
- Whether the child was being fostered by the prospective adopter.
- Whether the child was brought into the UK for adoption, including date of entry and whether an adoption order was made in the child's country of origin.
- Personality and social development, including emotional and behavioural development and any related needs.
- Details of interests, likes and dislikes.
- A summary, written by the agency's medical adviser, of the child's health history, their current state of health and any need for health care which is anticipated, and date of the most recent medical examination. NB – a health report from the medical adviser is not required if the child is placed by an agency or it is a step-parent adoption. In such cases a summary by the social worker of any significant matters will suffice.
- Any known learning difficulties or known general medical or mental health factors which are likely to have, or may have, genetic implications.
- Names, addresses and types of nurseries or schools attended, with dates.
- Educational attainments.

- Any special needs in relation to the child (whether physical, learning, behavioural or any other) and their emotional and behavioural development.
- Whether the child is subject to a statement under the Education Act 1996.
- Previous orders concerning the child:
  the name of the court;
  the order made; and
  the date of the order.
- Inheritance rights and any claim to damages under the Fatal Accidents Act 1976 the child stands to retain or lose if adopted.
- Any other relevant information which might assist the court.

ii) Each Parent of the Child

- Name, date and place of birth and address (date on which last address was confirmed current) including local authority area.
- Photograph, if available, and physical description.
- Nationality.
- Racial origin and cultural and linguistic background.
- Whether the mother and father were married to each other at the time of the child's birth or have subsequently married.
- Where the parent has been previously married or entered into a civil partnership, dates of those marriages or civil partnerships.
- Where the mother and father are not married, whether the father has parental responsibility and, if so, how it was acquired.
- If the identity or whereabouts of the father are not known, the information about him that has been ascertained and from whom, and the steps that have been taken to establish paternity.
- Past and present relationship with the other parent.
- Other information about the parent, where available:
  health, including any known learning difficulties or known general medical or mental health factors which are likely to have, or may have, genetic implications; religious persuasion; educational history; employment history; andpersonality and interests.
- Any other relevant information which might assist the court.

Part 2 - Relationships, contact arrangements and views

(i) The Child

- If the child is in the care of a local authority or voluntary organisation, or has been, details (including dates) of any placements with foster parents, or other arrangements in respect of the care of the child, including particulars of the persons with whom the child has had their home and observations on the care provided.
- The child's wishes and feelings (if appropriate, having regard to the child's age and understanding) about adoption, the application and its

consequences, including any wishes in respect of religious and cultural upbringing.

- The child's wishes and feelings in relation to contact (if appropriate, having regard to the child's age and understanding).
- The child's wishes and feelings recorded in any other proceedings.
- Date when the child's views were last ascertained.

(ii) The Child's Parents (or guardian) and relatives

- The parents' wishes and feelings before the placement, about the placement and about adoption, the application and its consequences, including any wishes in respect of the child's religious and cultural upbringing.
- Each parent's (or guardian's) wishes and feelings in relation to contact.
- Date/s when the views of each parent or guardian were last ascertained.
- Arrangements concerning any siblings, including half-siblings and step-siblings, and whether any are the subject of a parallel application or have been the subject of any orders. If so, for each case give: the name of the court; the order made, or (if proceedings are pending) the order applied for; the date of order, or date of next hearing if proceedings are pending.
- Extent of contact with the child's mother and father and, in each case, the nature of the relationship enjoyed.
- The relationship which the child has with relatives, and with any other person considered relevant, including:
  the likelihood of any such relationship continuing and the value to the child of its doing so; and the ability and willingness of any of the child's relatives, or of any such person, to provide the child with a secure environment in which the child can develop, and otherwise to meet the child's needs.
- The wishes and feelings of any of the child's relatives, or of any such person, regarding the child.
- Whether the parents (or members of the child's family) have met or are likely to meet the prospective adopter and, if they have met, the effect on all involved of such meeting.
- Dates when the views of members of the child's wider family and any other relevant person were last ascertained.

Part 3 - A summary of the actions of the adoption agency

- Brief account of the agency's actions in the case, with particulars and dates of all written information and notices given to the child and their parents and any person with parental responsibility.
- If consent has been given for the child to be placed for adoption, and also consent for the child to be adopted, the names of those who gave

consent and the date such consents were given. If such consents were subsequently withdrawn, the dates of these withdrawals.

- If any statement has been made under section 20(4)(a) of the Adoption and Children Act 2002 (the "2002 Act") that a parent or guardian does not wish to be informed of any application for an adoption order, the names of those who have made such statements and the dates the statements were made. If such statements were subsequently withdrawn, the dates of these withdrawals.
- Whether an order has been made under section 21 of the 2002 Act, section 18 of the Adoption (Scotland) Act 1978 or Article 17(1) or
- Brief details and dates of assessments of the child's needs, including expert opinions.
- Reasons for considering that adoption would be in the child's best interests (with date of relevant decision and reasons for any delay in implementing the decision).

Section C: The prospective adopter of the child
Part 1 - Information about the Prospective Adopter, including suitability to adopt

- Name, date and place of birth and address (date on which last address was confirmed current) including local authority area.
- Photograph and physical description.
- Whether the prospective adopter is domiciled or habitually resident in a part of the British Islands and, if habitually resident, for how long they have been habitually resident.
- Racial origin and cultural and linguistic background.
- Marital status or civil partnership status, date and place of most recent marriage (if any) or civil partnership (if any).
- Details of any previous marriage, civil partnership, or relationship where the prospective adopter lived with another person as a partner in an enduring family relationship.
- Relationship (if any) to the child.
- Where adopters wish to adopt as a couple, the status of the relationship and an assessment of the stability and permanence of their relationship.
- If a married person or a civil partner is applying alone, the reasons for this.
- Description of how the prospective adopter relates to adults and children.
- Previous experience of caring for children (including as a step-parent, foster parent, child-minder or prospective adopter) and assessment of ability in this respect, together where appropriate with assessment of ability in bringing up the prospective adopter's own children.

- A summary, written by the agency's medical adviser, of the prospective adopter's health history, current state of health and any need for health care which is anticipated, and date of most recent medical examination.
- Assessment of ability and suitability to bring up the child throughout their childhood.
- Details of income and comments on the living standards of the household with particulars of the home and living conditions (and particulars of any home where the prospective adopter proposes to live with the child, if different).
- Details of other members of the household, including any children of the prospective adopter even if not resident in the household.
- Details of the parents and any siblings of the prospective adopter, with their ages or ages at death.
- Other information about the prospective adopter: religious persuasion; educational history; employment history; and personality and interests.
- Confirmation that the applicants have not been convicted of, or cautioned for, a specified offence within the meaning of regulation 23(3) of the Adoption Agencies Regulations 2005 (S.I. 2005/389).
- Confirmation that the prospective adopter is still approved.
- Confirmation that any referees have been interviewed, with a report of their views and opinion of the weight to be placed thereon and whether they are still valid.
- Details of any previous family court proceedings in which the prospective adopter has been involved (which have not been referred to elsewhere in this report).

Part 2 - Wishes, views and contact arrangements

Prospective Adopter

- Whether the prospective adopter is willing to follow any wishes of the child or their parents or guardian in respect of the child's religious and cultural upbringing.
- The views of other members of the prospective adopter's household and wider family in relation to the proposed adoption.
- Reasons for the prospective adopter wishing to adopt the child and extent of understanding of the nature and effect of adoption. Whether the prospective adopter has discussed adoption with the child.
- Any hope and expectations the prospective adopter has for the child's future.
- The prospective adopter's wishes and feelings in relation to contact.

Part 3 - Actions of the adoption agency

- Brief account of the Agency's actions in the case, with particulars and dates of all written information and notices given to the prospective adopter.

- The Agency's proposals for contact, including options for facilitating or achieving any indirect contact or direct contact.
- The Agency's opinion on the likely effect on the prospective adopter and on the security of the placement of any proposed contact.
- Where the prospective adopter has been approved by an agency as suitable to be an adoptive parent, the agency's reasons for considering that the prospective adopter is suitable to be an adoptive parent for this child (with dates of relevant decisions).

Section D: The placement

- Where the child was placed for adoption by an adoption agency (section 18 of the 2002 Act), the date and circumstances of the child's placement with prospective adopter.
- Where the child is living with persons who have applied for the adoption order to be made (section 44 of the 2002 Act), the date when notice of intention to adopt was given.
- Where the placement is being provided with adoption support, this should be summarised and should include the plan and timescales for continuing the support beyond the making of the adoption order.
- Where the placement is not being provided with adoption support, the reasons why.
- A summary of the information obtained from the Agency's visits and reviews of the placement, including whether the child has been seen separately to the prospective adopter and whether there has been sufficient opportunity to see the family group and the child's interaction in the home environment.
- An assessment of the child's integration within the family of the prospective adopter and the likelihood of the child's full integration into the family and community.
- Any other relevant information that might assist the court.

Section E: Recommendations

- The relative merits of adoption and other orders with an assessment of whether the child's long term interests would be best met by an adoption order or by other orders (such as residence and special guardianship orders).
- Recommendations as to whether or not the order sought should be made (and, if not, alternative proposals).
- Recommendations as to whether there should be future contact arrangements (or not) and the nature of any such arrangements.

Appendix 5

Useful contact details

Local Government Ombudsman

Advice line: 0845 602 1983
www.lgo.org.uk

Information Commissioner's Office

Promotes access to official information and protects personal information.

Information Commissioner's Office
– England
Wycliffe House, Water Lane,
Wilmslow, Cheshire SK9 5AF
Helpline: 01625 545 745
Email: mail@ico.gsi.gov.uk
www.informationcommissioner.gov.uk

Information Commissioner's Office
– Wales
2 Alexandra Gate, Ffordd Pengam,
Cardiff CF24 2SA
Tel: 02920 894 929
Email: wales@ico.gsi.gov.uk

Her Majesty's Court Service

www.hmcourts-service.gov.uk
Website has list of all County Court
Adoption Centres.

Government departments responsible for adoption

England

Department for Education and Skills
Looked After Children Division

Caxton House, Tothill Street,
London SW1H 9NA
Tel: 0870 000 2288
Email: info@dfes.gsi.gov.uk
www.dfes.gov.uk/adoption

Department for Trade and Industry
Response Centre, 1 Victoria Street,
London SW1H 0ET
Tel: 020 7215 5000
Email: dti.enquiries@dti.gsi.gov.uk
www.dti.gov.uk/workingparents
www.tiger.gov.uk

Wales

The National Assembly for Wales
Children and Families Division
Cathays Park, Cardiff CF10 3NQ
Tel: 029 2082 3676
www.wales.gov.uk

Adoption Contact Register

England and Wales
The Office for National Statistics,
General Register Office, Adoptions
Section, Smedley Hydro, Trafalgar
Road, Southport, Merseyside PR8 2HH
Tel: 0151 471 4830
Email: adoptions@ons.gsi.gov.uk
www.gro.gov.uk

Adoption Register for England and Wales

Unit 4, Pavilion Business Park,
Royds Hall Road, Wortley, Leeds
LS12 6AJ
Tel: 0870 750 2173
Helpline: 0870 750 2176
Email: mail@adoptionregister.org.uk

Independent Review Mechanism

IRM Contract Manager
Dolphin House, 54 Coventry Road,
Birmingham B10 0RX
Tel: 0121 766 8086
Email: irm@baaf.org.uk
www.irm-adoption.org.uk

Sources of legal advice

Family Rights Group
The Print House, 18 Ashwin Street,
London E8 3DL
Advice line: 0800 731 1696
Email: advice@frg.org.uk

Resolution - first for family law
PO Box 302, Orpington, Kent BR6 8QX
Tel: 01689 820272
Email: info@resolution.org.uk

The Children's Legal Centre
University of Essex, Wivenhoe Park,
Colchester, Essex CO4 3SQ
Tel: 01206 872 466
Advice line: 0845 456 6811
Email: clc@essex.ac.uk

Recommended Reading

Making sense of the New Adoption Law Nick Allen, Russell House Publishing, 2003.

Making sense of the Children Act 1989 Nick Allen, 4th Ed, John Wiley and Sons Ltd, 2005.
Includes amendments made by the Adoption and Children Act 2002 and the Children Act 2004.

Adoption Now – Current Law including Regulations and Guidance Fergus Smith and Deborah Cullen, BAAF, 2nd Ed, 2006.
Incorporates changes brought about by the Adoption and Children Act 2002 and the Civil Partnership Act 2004.

Child Care Law – A summary of the Law in England and Wales Deborah Cullen and Mary Lane, BAAF, 5th Ed, 2006.
Incorporating changes brought about by the Adoption and Children Act 2002, the Children Act 2004 and the Civil Partnership Act 2004.

Adoption and Fostering BAAF quarterly journal.

The Adopter's Handbook: Information, resources and services for adoptive parents Amy Neil Salter, BAAF, 2006.

What happens in court? - A guide for children Hedi Argent and Mary Lane, BAAF, 2004.

Child friendly explanations about the courts when care orders, placement orders or adoption orders are applied for.

Appendix 6

List of County Court Adoption Centres

Aberystwyth	Chester	Manchester	Romford
Birmingham	Coventry	Medway	Sheffield
Blackburn	Croydon	Middlesbrough	Southampton
Bolton	Derby	Milton Keynes	Stockport
Bournemouth	Exeter	Newcastle	Stoke-On-Trent
Bow	Guildford	Newport	Sunderland
Bradford	Ipswich	Northampton	Swansea
Brentford	Kingston-Upon-Hull	Norwich	Swindon
Brighton	Lancaster	Nottingham	Taunton
Bristol	Leeds	Oxford	Teesside
Bromley	Leicester	Peterborough	Telford
Cambridge	Lincoln	Plymouth	Truro
Canterbury	Liverpool	Pontypridd	Warrington
Cardiff	Llangefni	Portsmouth	Watford
Carlisle	Luton	Reading	Wolverhampton
Chelmsford	Macclesfield	Rhyl	Worcester
York			

London and South East applications

Applications for adoption orders can also be made to the Principal
Registry of the Family Division in The Strand, which also functions
as a county court, and is the adoption centre for central London.
However legal advice should be taken upon whether this is the
appropriate court in view of the likelihood of considerable delay in
applications being listed for hearing at such a busy County Court.

Index